The University of Life

Jimmy McKenzie

Published by New Generation Publishing in 2013

Copyright © Jimmy McKenzie 2013

First Edition

The author asserts the moral right under the Copyright, Designs and Patents Act 1988 to be identified as the author of this work.

All Rights reserved. No part of this publication may be reproduced, stored in a retrieval system or transmitted, in any form or by any means without the prior consent of the author, nor be otherwise circulated in any form of binding or cover other than that which it is published and without a similar condition being imposed on the subsequent purchaser.

www.newgeneration-publishing.com

 **New Generation Publishing**

Dedicated to the memories and much cherished times with Auntie Mary and Uncle Davie. "Gone are the voices we loved to hear, gone are the faces we loved so dear."

Acknowledgments

Thanks to the best mum and dad a son could ask for, and for also keeping my feet firmly on the ground. Thanks to Aileen, amazing sister, and Peter, for making me appear to be the normal, quieter sibling. Thanks to the three amazing lecturers I had at college, they continue to be very good friends and mentors, along will all the wonderful characters I have met on building sites and worked with. Thanks to Ogilvie Group, and Tom, for pulling me out and showing me a future just when I needed it. Thanks to my Auntie Mary for showing me a lifestyle ethos I try to adhere to everyday. Thank you to all my friends, old and new, who all think they are safe now - beware, this is only the beginning, and many of you have supplied me with excellent material. A special thank you to my beautiful daughter Charlie, who continues to amaze and scare me at the same time, and of course "the gingers", who continue to make life challenging. A special thank you to my beloved Sarah, with whom I have finally met my match.

Divine Intervention?

The clouds above were shaped like a trumpet wielding guardsman, the smell in the air was of freshly cut grass, the sun was warming my skin nicely. I felt as if I was in a fabric conditioner advert off the television. One of those memories which seemed incidental at the time, but would stay with me forever, for my whole life time. Even now when I shut my eyes I can almost transcend back to that day at the back of the sports centre, in Denny.

Me, and two of my best mates had been hanging around, kicking a ball about, and generally slagging each other off and more importantly slagging other people off. It was the summer of 1995, we had just left school and were at that glorious time, which still sends tingles down my spine – The start of the summer holidays! We had spent the day messing around, idly wasting time as if it was endless. Doing nothing at all with our day apart from seeing who could be triumphant in the "friendly put-down" stakes, to which I always felt confident. Craig and Chris were, and still are, two of my best mates. With the addition of Colin, these are three guys who have been my mates for a very long time, and for the foreseeable future. I didn't at that time realise the significance of that day, but it was to become one of the most poignant shaping moments of my life. We were lying at the foot of the large tree which sits at the side of the 5 a side football pitch, talking about what our plans would be for the summer and beyond. My mind was thinking that I just wanted to not think about the future, I was just happy chilling out in the moment, living for the there and then, and not worrying about what comes next. But, alas, every moment of thought eventually ends, and the next one begins.

This was the moment where I was about to come to a decision which would shape the rest of my life... I sat bolt upright, and the words which would follow, I was to regret many times in the coming years. Words which were to send shivers of fear through my parents bodies. A moment where I encountered a cross roads in life, and only hoped I had made the right decision.

"fuck it! I've decided, I'm no going to Uni"

As soon as the words left my mouth I almost regretted saying them! The friends I was with were fairly unmoved by my decision. I had kind of hoped they would promote drama and talk me out of the decision. Probably because Craig had been unemployed for a few months, Chris was working a summer job as an electrician before heading to college to start a course in Graphic Design. My decision was to not attend University, which was due to begin in around two months' time. I was scheduled, so long as I got the passes I required in my Higher Exams, to attend Robert Gordon University, in Aberdeen, to study a degree in hospitality management. The previous winter I had been persuaded that Uni was the way to go. Since my childhood dreams of becoming a footballer had fallen by the way side, and I had been put off architecture by a brief stint of work experience from school at the architect offices at Falkirk Council, a fate which had also scuppered my idea of becoming an electrician, I had decided that I would continue my education, until I finally found something that I wanted to do for the rest of my life. That meant the arduous conquest of filling out meaningless applications, pretending to study for the Highers I had promised to pass. No easy task, but one which I took to without too much trouble.

I wasn't a naturally talented or academically gifted kid. I generally was pretty average at everything I did. Be it sports, school work, general brightness etc. I was probably in the "easily forgotten" group. As a teacher would think, the students remembered are generally the really talented ones, the really un-talented ones, and the downright daft or weird ones. Otherwise, the "average Joe's" just fall into the category where they didn't stick out for any particular reason, therefore they kind of just fade into the past. That was probably the group I was in. I held my own at Sports, Art, English, Maths, and pretty much every other subject at school, nothing really inspired me, but I was good enough that I was persuaded with a bit more effort I could go to university. The only problem was, to do what?

That previous winter I had thumbed through the UCAS application book, found a course which seemed to have obtainable requirements in terms of exam passes, and decided on a wing, that I was going to be a hospitality manager type dude! Did I actually know what that was? No. Did I actually know what it entailed? No. Was I really interested in being a manager in the hospitality industry? Probably not! But, hey-ho, it meant I was off to Uni to consider my next move, whilst pleasing my parents by making them proud of me. That was something that made me at least warm slightly to the idea.

So, back to behind the sports centre on that sunny July day. I had abruptly come to the decision that I was not going to go to Aberdeen. I made a snap decision based on what? I didn't fancy moving away from home, didn't much fancy studying something I wasn't interested in, was having a nice wee summer hanging around with my mates down the Park. Ach fuck it, I thought, something will turn up! As a saying which has served me well throughout my life, I just told myself "one door shuts, another one will open." And as it turned out that other door was about to open sooner than I thought.

The rest of that afternoon, I put the thought of my career out of my mind and tried to make the most of enjoying myself. We ended up going to the garage for juice then down to Craig's parents' house to play his guitar and listen to music. After a few hours I decided to head home as it was nearing tea time. When I arrived at my folks' house my Dad had been out cutting the grass and my mum was in the kitchen. My folks were always very supportive of anything I did, and still are. I come from a very small family; my parents had just myself and my older sister. I didn't know any of my grandparents. I don't have a single cousin as both my parents were the only kids in their families to have children. We were always, and still are, a very close family. It's possibly because there aren't many of us. My mum had three sisters and a brother. They were brought up on a farm, and still had a lot of typical farming values, I was virtually brought up on the farm as well, I was very close to my aunties and uncle. On 9th December 2010 when the fire burned down, my closest auntie and uncle were in it. This was a very sad time for my already small family. My dad's side of the family was also very small. He has a sister, but they don't speak often. I don't really know her, having only met her when I was a kid. My folks worked very hard, and even though they are retired now, they still work hard. They constantly amaze me. My Dad was a HGV lorry driver most of his working life, having worked for the same company for over 40 years. My mum returned to working in a bank when we were old enough to go to school. Life was a struggle when we were young, but my sister and I never went without, even though they did. I think things were a bit easier later in life, but I sensed their pride when I announced I was planning to attend university. I can imagine this was the feeling they would've felt because life was tough, and they would've been so happy to see me making my way in the world myself. That feeling probably wasn't too long lived. I got the feeling my mum especially would be a bit disappointed at my new plans, or lack thereof.

As I usually told myself, one of my favourite sayings, "one door shuts, another one opens" was fairly well played out. That day when I got home my dad had been out the back cutting the grass. He had been speaking to a neighbour, Davie Tinnie, who stayed two doors down from us. Davie owned a small Painting and Decorating business. He was a middle aged man, who had stayed there all my life. I didn't know much about him other than that he was our neighbour, and ran a business from his house. My mum and dad mentioned him sometimes, and I think they also knew his two daughters. He sometimes painted my house in the summer, and he seemed to be a nice man. Well, as luck would have it, he had been telling my dad how he had just won a large contract to paint a brand new block of flats in Glasgow. My dad must've been telling him how I was a bit unsettled and unsure of my future. Well, low and behold, Davie mentioned he was thinking of taking on a couple of apprentices and wondered if I fancied a start! Possibly not my first choice of a trade if I was to become an apprentice in anything, but it was certainly an option! Would I want to be a Painter and Decorator? Would I be any good as a painter and decorator? Would I be willing to give up a place at University to work a trade? This was going to have to take some thought....

After a couple of days of talking about it and mentioning it to a couple of people, I was of the opinion, how difficult could it be? It was painting. Surely couldn't be that hard?? I had a vision of standing in the sun, nice and warm, with the sun on my back, painting away at a wall. Surely I wasn't underestimating this?! Could I be? And as for the thought of giving up a university education for a trade; I had convinced myself that money in the pocket each week was much more valuable than an empty promise of a "good job" after completing a degree. It seemed to me the world was full of educated folk who couldn't get work at the required level.

So, after researching it fully to the furthest degree, I decided a life as a Painter and Decorator was going to be just the ticket. It was a trade after all, something I could take anywhere in the world, or have my own business. Hey, that sounded amazing, the sky's the limit! I'll be a millionaire in no time, I thought!

Starting Work

My first day at work was one of surprises. I was a little nervous, and a whole lot excited. My dad, who made his sandwiches the night before for his work, took great pride in also making my lunch. I could almost feel his pride. His youngest kid, only son, was off to begin work. A major step in the road to becoming a man! I was 17, had not long passed my driving test, and had the world at my feet! That night, I felt a sense of pride also. I would be able to pay "Dig Money" to my Mum for my share of the house-keeping, it genuinely felt like I was taking a step towards manhood! I went to bed, having laid out clothes and boots, finding a bag for my lunch, and setting my alarm for early the next morning.

I bounced out of bed the next morning as soon as the alarm sounded. I got ready and dressed in no time, and was sat watching TV with a half hour to spare. When the time was right I gave my Mum a kiss and headed outside to wait for Davie. I waited nervously at the bus stop across from my house. The agreement was that Davie would go and pick up one of his men, then come and get me. I assumed I'd be working with Davie all day, something that reassured me slightly as I kind of knew him, and he knew my folks. As I stood, a couple minutes had passed by the agreed time; I saw his van coming over the brow of the hill. I was feeling pretty nervous now. I kept telling myself I would manage this. I suddenly wondered if I was wearing the correct clothing. Nothing had been mentioned by Davie, but I just assumed old clothes would be wise as we would be painting. The van pulled up, and Davie signalled me to climb in. Sliding across from the window seat to the middle seat was Ally, Davie's top worker, I would soon learn. I shook his hand when we were introduced, and sat quietly. Davie and Ally discussed the work of the day, and I spoke when spoken to. I suddenly felt like a little boy again, in a big man's world! Davie explained that I wouldn't be working with him at all that day; I was going with Ally, to Glasgow, in another van from the main contractor's yard at Kilsyth. So, straight away I was being removed from any sight of comfort zone that I may have imagined. We arrived at Kilsyth, and Ally hurriedly urged me to help him shift bags of plaster into the back of another van, hastily tossed onto the floor of the van, which had a wooden bench along each side of the back compartment. When we were finished, Davie drove away and Ally ushered me into the van and onto a bench. We sat as the driver pulled away and I felt a bag of plaster slide over onto my foot. Sitting in the back of a van, along with materials, was perfectly normal back in these days, something you would go to jail for now! As we drove along through roads I had never been before, no one speaking, I felt very uncomfortable, as I was completely in the unknown. I didn't know the guy sitting with me, I didn't know the driver up front, or where he was taking us. At least there was only Ally and myself in the back of the van. As we drove through a small town the driver was blethering away in the front with the passenger, Ally and I were sat in silence in the back. I was watching out the front window trying to make out some landmarks that I may recognise. Suddenly the van pulled up, the back door opened, and one of the largest men I have ever seen was standing at the door. With a "Mornin' boys" he jumped in and sat directly across from me. He was huge, both tall and wide, a real bear of a man. He had dark hair and a moustache, and looked like he would be able to pick me up with one hand and crush me like an insect. Now I was feeling really intimidated. This was turning into an eye opening experience. The van trundled on for a few hundred yards until we stopped again, and again the door swung open to reveal another visually intimidating character. This time, a tall slimmer guy, with a shaved head. I'll be honest and say, probably even more terrifying than the first. I got a first impression that he looked like a skin-head throwback from the 70's. I thought to myself, I'm really in at the deep end, this is going to be interesting! Further along the way, we stopped another 2 or three times, picking up all shapes and sizes of men, all who knew each other and were speaking about how their weekends had been. Mostly the stories involved drunkenness, drugs, and fighting. There was plentiful supply of colourful language. I just sat, frozen to my seat, listening and glancing at them occasionally. No one took any notice of me. It was one of those situations where you are in a dentist or doctors waiting room, there are a few people waiting, some reading a magazine, some talking on their mobile phone, some just sitting. I reckon that if i'm in that situation, I could be sat for ten minutes....months later I might pass by a person in the high street, and I will recognise them from a particular time or waiting room. I feel that is an amazing skill, maybe everyone can do it? I don't know. But I put it down to collecting football stickers as a kid, Panini '86 and the like. Swapping large piles of stickers at lunchtimes with mates. It's left me with almost photographic memory for faces. Well this situation was like that, after that van journey I would, and could've, and have, remembered those faces my whole life! I was in a van full of *men,* I felt merely a boy against them. As I sat, listening intently, I could've easily not have been there and no one would've noticed any different.

Eventually, we pulled up to the job. It was a building site located at Charing Cross in Glasgow. Everyone jumped out of the van and headed away in to the site. Ally and I started to lift the bags of plaster, which by now were squashed looking and covered in some huge footprints. Ally instructed me to pile them at the gate entrance, which we did before the driver went and parked the van. We then took the first couple along with our bags, and I followed Ally into the building. The heavy plaster bag over my shoulder and my lunch bag in hand, I tried my best to walk over the rocky, rubble surface in Ally's steps. The stage of the construction of the building was fairly early. It was basically a shell of a building. The staircase we were climbing up was finished only in rough blockwork, no front door, just an opening. As we climbed the stairs, and turned back round to face another set, I could feel my legs getting tired. It was only half past 8 in the morning and my legs were burning already. When we eventually reached the top it seemed a little further developed than the lower floors. In all there were 4 floor levels. Ally trudged along a hallway, bag of plaster over his shoulder, and piece bag in hand. We passed by various men, in different colours of overalls, and with different tools and equipment at work. Each one glanced at me as if to recognise I was "new meat". He turned into what I assumed was a flat doorway, and into a side room, where he dumped the bag on the floor. By this point my thighs were burning, I dropped the bag beside his. He looked at me and smiled "cumoan wee man, only another 8 bags to go". I was thinking to myself, can we go home after this?! After we eventually got the bags upstairs to the "howf", Ally pulled a white pair of overalls from his bag and threw them to me. "They're Davie's auld yins, they'll be big on ye, but they'll do 'til we see if yer gonnae stick it or no". Ally picked up a pair from the corner of the howf and started pulling them on. I unravelled the overalls and pulled them over my boots. "Right, so, you want tae be a painter?" "Well... I think so" I quivered back. It was clear to me, that I had a lot of growing up and toughening up to do if I wanted to make it in this world. I found out in the space of an hour I was very wet behind the ears, when previously, as I have found out, like all 17 year olds, I thought I was pretty on top of my game. Well, let the learning begin, I just hope Ally was up for it.

At that time Ally was 23. I found that out once we started talking while working. The first couple of days I think he was sussing me out. I later realised that he must've been told by Davie that I was the son of a mate, so he must've been apprehensive that I was going to be a grass and let slip any wrong doings to the boss. I can now understand the initial coldness! Ally was a laid back natured guy, still lived with his folks too, had a girlfriend and car, and liked to enjoy himself at the weekends. I could tell even by his work clothes that he kept himself trendy, his old work clothes consisted of Lacoste jumpers or polo's, smart jeans, and timberland boots that had seen better days. Clearly image was pretty important to Ally, he was clean shaven, with neat blond hair, probably about 5'11", and of slim build. I'm not quite sure what he thought of me, at that time I was kind of stuck in between two images. I was a bit chubby still from youth, and was in between trendy and the whole Grunge look of the early nineties. Think i'd just try and pass that off as a poor supply of old working gear! I hadn't truly found my look, and i'm sticking to that story. I'm only grateful there are virtually no pictures of me from that time! That first day flew by, Ally showed me how to do the nail hole filling, the very easiest task that he could find for me, while he wielded a hawk and trowel like a master!

We had a couple of tea breaks and a half hour lunch break. Ally had a bottle of Irn-Bru and his pieces, I had what looked like a lunch that was packed by my mum! Mental note; tomorrow, buy a bottle of juice from the shop, and have a manlier looking lunch! No more "Capri-Sun's" for me, I'm a big boy now! During the lunch time Ally asked a little about me. Just the basics. But it was a sign that he was at least showing an interest in me. The lunch and tea were pretty strictly on time as Ally was clearly a good worker. He showed enthusiasm and skill with his tools, but in a cool way which was easy for a younger, impressionable kid to admire. I spent a lot of the day just watching Ally using the hawk and trowel. Apparently this technique was called "Aimes Taping" – a method used to disguise the plasterboard joints in walls and ceilings. He was clearly good at it, but what did I know?! I was keen to learn, so I asked questions as and when they came into my head, something I have always done. I always think that no matter whom or what comes into your life there's always something that you can learn from them. When I ran out of questions about taping, I would ask Ally about his life. I could tell he was being very cagey about what he told me, but I just kept asking. I think he probably began to open up to me because he was sick of trying to think of what he should and shouldn't tell me! Working with Ally made me feel like I wanted to learn more about this strange old business of painting and decorating. After a day with him I thought he was a cool guy. He made painting and decorating seem like a very cool job to have. Looking back, if it wasn't for Ally taking me under his wing that first day, then I probably would never have kept at it. Something that I will forever hold against him! After that first day of work we jumped back into the van. I was totally buzzing. I felt a real inner pride. I had completed my first day of work in the big bad world of work! I probably hadn't accomplished much, except for filling a few hundred nail holes, but I showed I was keen, willing to learn, and reliable (I hoped).I had got into the back of that van that morning, an intimidated, vulnerable boy. This time I was getting in it as a man, a working man. Albeit, I had earned £9- one fifth of my vast weekly wage of £45! Although I had a new found level of manhood, as soon as I sat back in the van I soon reverted back to my little boy mode. The bear like, thuggish labourers who had intimidated me that morning, were such strong characters that it was very difficult to be any different around them. They were a close knit pack. Ally also kept himself to himself in the van. So for the journey back to Kilsyth, it was back to looking at my shoes again with the odd glance at whoever was holding court at the time. And this time I didn't even have a bag of plaster at my feet to read.

The journey seemed to be over a lot quicker this time. I was trying to grasp some sort of figuring on what type of people these guys were, who was the top dog amongst them, who was the "victim" in there. They seemed fascinating to me. The stories they told, the way they told them, the way they interacted with each other. One of the older labourers, probably around early 50's was sat directly across from me. To this day, one of the funniest, innocently funny, things to watch is a human being fighting sleep. Be it in a meeting, a classroom, a car or even a baby in a high chair on TV, the vision of someone fighting sleep just cracks me up in a laugh-out –loud kind of way. So, the older guy was sitting across from me, on glancing up I noticed his eyes beginning to roll back. He was clearly in that not quite conscious, not yet asleep stage, usually affected by the inability to get completely comfortable. I could certainly appreciate that in a cramped, sweaty, uncomfortable van, surrounded by 6-8 absolute gorillas of men. His head was rolling forward quickly enough to momentarily wake him slightly, but the second his head went back I was drawn to see the show. It was like witnessing a man fighting against himself, an internal struggle between good and evil, a fight he was never going to win. It was like watching a boxing match on TV, he was fighting hard against it. I fought hard to keep my laugh in, "look away, look away" I told myself. Once his head flew forward so hard he nearly headbutted his own knee. I let out a stifled grunty laugh, which I was quick enough to disguise with a couple of throat clearing coughs. Ooft that was close. I really could do without getting on the wrong side of any of these men! I told myself that's enough for one day, back to looking at feet. As we got closer to the yard, one by one, the labourers were dropped off at various points, each saying farewell to their workmates before jumping out. Before long it was just Ally and I in the back. When we arrived back at the yard, Davie was waiting in his van to pick us up. After the day I had, it was almost like being greeted by a long lost pal, a familiar face, I was glad to see him. On the journey back he asked how I had got on and if I enjoyed it. I could tell he wasn't really listening to what I was saying, but he tuned right in to Ally's answers when he asked him how I was that day. The journey back home wasn't long, I was glad because I was quite excited to tell my parents of the day's events – and how I was going to be the best Painter and Decorator that had ever lived!

Over the next few days, Ally started to realise that I was no threat to him. We used to walk up to the shop at lunchtime. Ally loved to go for a wee walk when all the office girls were out for lunch, and I must say I wasn't too averse to it either. We'd sit and eat our lunch and watch the world go by. It was great. The sun was out, it was warm, and there was loads of life about the city, hustle bustle with people going about their lives. It was from this time that I probably blame for my constant habit of people watching. I think it's fascinating to watch strangers going about their business, and to try and imagine what sort of life they have. Are they married? If so, do they rule their world or are they brow beaten spouse pleasers'? Even imagining what these city folk did for jobs, the possibilities were endless. I could see Ally was also very much a people person. I liked his enthusiasm for life, especially life outside work. We used to talk a lot while working. Quite often I would work side by side with Ally. We would talk about random things that came up. This would be some of the most inspirational conversations that I would ever have. I didn't really realise it at the time, but one of the most poignant lessons that I learnt from this time was that no matter who you encounter in life, you can learn from them. Be it a homeless person you stop to buy a "Big Issue" from, or an MP who visits your work place, the beauty about human beings is that the possibilities and life experience is so much vaster than anything that a single person can comprehend.

Some of the conversations we had have stuck with me forever, and some I have kept and used myself in certain situations. I could relate well to Ally as he was only 7 years older than me. He was on a similar mind-set to what I was, and what I wanted to be. As I was keen to learn, and knew I wanted to be good at what I did, I took every day as a learning opportunity alongside him, he was a perfect role model for me at that time. He worked hard, played harder, and looked to take the simple pleasures from every part of his life. Adopting that ethos was going to be great for me, so I went about changing my mind-set forever.

As part of my apprenticeship, I would be attending college after the summer. One of Ally's stories was that he had won the "Apprentice of the Year" award when he was at college; this had made Davie an extremely proud boss. He was almost seen as the "chosen one" of all Davie's employees. This went a long way to Ally being held in such high regard, and Davie trusting, and speaking highly of him, at every opportunity. Ally was never a boastful type of person, quite the opposite in fact, but I knew that he was held in very high regard. I decided at that point that I was going to have to emulate his success at college, if not better it. How I would do that I wasn't yet sure, but it was something I now had in my sights, something to aim for!

One becomes two

Davie had decided that due to the magnitude of his upcoming jobs list that he wanted to take on another apprentice. Naturally, Davie was in a handy situation, he had on his books someone that had pals in exactly the same situation; me! This would save him money on advertising and other costs, he would have someone who was recommended to him, and more importantly, it gave me a chance to shine in his eyes. But I was fully aware that this was a precocious position for me to be in. Davie, being a clever businessman, gave me the opportunity to refer a couple of pals for interviews, with one of them hopefully getting the position of Apprentice Painter and Decorator, alongside me. So, firstly, I was looking after my own position, I didn't want someone getting the gig who was going to totally outshine me in Davie's, and also Ally's eyes, but If he hired a dummy, it would potentially make me look bad. This was going to have to be given some careful thought!

Which of my mates would fall into such a category? Who would be interested in following me into Painting? I put the news around my closest friends. Some of them I discounted straight away, whether due to poor work attitude, crazy late timekeeping at school, or just that they never bothered going at all. Most of them already had plans for post-school education of some sort, but Craig was currently unemployed and pretty keen on it. Also keen was Ryan, one of my closest friends from as far back as early primary school, probably from about 6 or 7 years old. I was happy for either of them to get the job alongside me. In a purely selfish attitude, both were good guys, I got on well with both, I knew them as well as was possible, and I didn't think I would be completely outshone by either. That may sound a little disrespectful, it's not intended to be, but if this master plan was to be put into action, I couldn't afford to have it collapse at the first hurdle.

So, both guys were put forward for interview. It was almost like two boxers squaring up to each other, pre-fight. Nose to nose, eyeballing each other looking for a weakness in their opponent. Because they were both good mates of mine, but not so much of each other, I had spent time in both of their company before the interviews. Let's be honest, their "trash-talk" wasn't the best! Ryan claimed he would be the best choice for the job because he had studied Craft and Design at school, where as part of a project, he had designed and built a miniature pool table. This pool table was made from wood and was around 200mm long. He had crafted tiny little pool cues and even smaller balls to play it with. Completely ridiculous looking back, but he assured me he was taking this "masterpiece" to his interview, to show off to his prospective new employer as a symbol of his amazing hand skills! It made me laugh hysterically the thought of him sitting in a waiting area, holding a miniature pool table! Even more so, of him showing Davie how to play with a pool cue the size of a tooth pick! This, he thought, would win the day for him, as Craig hadn't been too much involved in Craft and Design at school. I could appreciate Ryan's choice of approach, playing the hand skills card, talking up his history using tools and materials, but I wasn't sure about taking the pool table, surely showing his certificate would be enough?

Craig's argument and manifesto was much simpler. Craig proclaimed that because of the nature of the job, there was only one deciding factor in his eyes, to separate the two candidates. And what was this obvious decider? I tried to imagine feats or skills which he could boast of that would outshine a miniature pool table? Eventually he let out with... "I am taller than Ryan. It will be easier for me to paint up high!" After hearing that, the vision of Ryan sitting clasping a miniature pool table seemed a little less ridiculous... I had always seen Craig as a fairly bright lad as well.

The interviews were to be held one evening, after work, at Davie's house. I couldn't help myself peering out my mum's living room window at the time for the interviews. The mere sight of Ryan with the pool table would be enough to set me off laughing, and he didn't disappoint. Not only that, he arrived in suitable attire, of a knitted "Pringle" jumper, and smart trousers. Craig on the other hand arrived in a shirt and trousers which clearly looked borrowed- A knack that Craig has perfected over the years. I swear, he could be dressed in an "Armani" suit that boy, and still look a mess. This in later years would be perfected in the "un-ironed look" which literally meant him going out in clothes straight from the washing basket! He was the butt of endless jokes, when he'd walk into the pub with jeans and shirt clearly not ironed, and the rest of us dressed to impress. So, after the interviews, the next morning, no one had heard who had got the job, apprenticeship, and possible stepping stone to a new career. Davie picked me up as normal, Ally in his usual seat, off we set to Kilsyth to get the other van. I didn't want to ask, but was desperate to know how they had faired. Had Craig suitably impressed Davie and Ally with his slightly taller than average "height", or had the miniature, fairy sized, pool table been too overwhelming to ignore? I was buzzing to find out.

Davie let me know fairly soon that the pigmy pool table had, in fact, been too overwhelming. Davie thought it showed initiative to bring along a sample of his handy work. Ally later shared with me that he had to look away when Ryan pulled it out, to avoid laughing. Anyway, none the less, Ryan had won an apprenticeship with me. We had always been quite competitive with each other, but really good pals, so I was really happy for him. And I knew he wouldn't let himself down. Craig, at the time, was a little disappointed, but picked himself up, and moved on. Craig is still a very close friend of mine, at time of writing this he has settled down with a lovely wife Catriona, and they have two beautiful daughters, with another child on the way. He eventually went to work in a local computer factory, and has done very well for himself.

Ryan was due to start at the beginning of the next week, so he was eager to get any info out of me about who he'd be working with. I probably wasn't that great a help to him as I'd only been there a week myself, and had only worked with Ally. I knew Davie had a business partner and a few other tradesmen, but I still hadn't met them. I was feeling pretty happy that I'd have a mate alongside me sometimes as, truth being told, I was a bit overwhelmed at times. The money wasn't exactly the big attraction to the job, 1st year wages of £45 per week. Davie assured me this would increase to £78 in second year. The four year apprenticeship seemed like a mammoth task to take on, but I was looking forward to it. Ally had told me that an apprentice attended college, on block release basis, for first and second year. Third year was optional, with the fourth year being completed as a full year on site. I was intrigued about the "optional" year. Ally explained that this was "Advanced Craft"- the units made up of the more fancy work like marbling, graining, gilding etc. I had made a pledge that I was going to be the best;

therefore I would have to complete this "Advanced Craft" malarkey.... I didn't even know what marbling and gilding were, but I wanted to know. I chose my moment carefully, and asked Davie if he was willing to put me through the full three years of college. He was due grants and benefits and stuff, but he still had to pay for my time up front, only getting the funding if I passed. He agreed. But only if I showed I was keen and worked hard. Thank you very much! I was on my way!

So, in no time at all Ryan and I had settled into a working life. We were both enjoying being "working men" and we had a good friendship both in and outside work. We were naturally pretty competitive with each other, and I would say it actually enhanced our progression. We both wanted to be top dog in Davie's eyes, and we both wanted to do well, which could only benefit the company. That full summer we were both working ahead of attending college in the autumn. The Glasgow job at Charing Cross progressed into having just painting work. Davie's partner Matt eventually also joined us, as did Davie, and the other guys who worked with Matt's squad. They were a bunch of guys who came from very mixed backgrounds, but were also very interesting, and I was to learn loads from them. Not just about P&D, but about life in general.

The first time I encountered Matt and his squad was on a bank holiday. Davie and Ally were having the day off, but Matt and his team were working as usual. I was told to be at my usual pick up point at my usual time, but Matt would pick me up. There I was waiting for another big shiny Mercedes van to pull up. I was a bit confused when standing at the bus stop, a clapped out old Ford Sierra estate car began slowing down as it approached. A moustached man in the driver's position signalled to me to get in the back seat. I opened the door and jumped in. "I take it you're Jimmy?" said

Matt. "I am. Hiya." Matt was around the same age as Davie, maybe a bit younger. I was a bit surprised at the so called works vehicle. I fully expected another big van, fully kitted out with tools and equipment. It was a sign of Matt's status within the firm, and with Davie, which I would soon learn more about.

Matt had four guys who worked mainly with him. One guy in his early 30's, one around Ally's age, and two older men. Callum was Matt's equivalent to Ally. Young, on top of his game, and respected by the workers. Joe was around thirty, fairly lazy, as in he would love to skive rather than work. I learned a lot from both guys, and eventually joined the same amateur football team they played in. The two older men were slightly different. One was one of the nicest men you could ever meet in life – Davie Mullen- more of a "Brush Hand" rather than an all-round tradesman. But, a good worker, wise in his ways, and an expert at cheering people up on a cold Monday morning. Davie Mullen was an absolute gem of a man, and I was to learn a lot of stuff from him, more about DIY car care and football, rather than painting.

As Matt drove along the road, I tried in vain to make light conversation. He was taking me to pick up the other men and then presumably onto a job. Passing through Banknock, he indicated to turn into a layby beside a shop. "Do you read a paper?" he asked. This obviously meant this was his traditional pick up point for a newspaper and any provisions he needed for the day. As we drew in, I noticed a stockily built man reading a Daily Record, leaning against the shop wall. As we pulled up, he growled a look towards the car and closed his paper. I got out walking towards the shop and the well built man glared at me as I passed him. My immediate impression was that of uneasiness. I felt a negative vibe coming from him right away. I had faced up to the scary labourers from the last couple of weeks on the Glasgow job, and had survived; surely I wasn't to meet anyone more intimidating than them. After buying my paper and bottle of Irn-Bru I headed back out to the car. There was another strange face sitting in the front passenger seat, with the stern faced man in the back. I jumped in, and assumed the old shoe staring position which served me well from the Glasgow van. When I got in the car I had my piece bag and my overalls which were rolled up. Because the angry faced man was now in the car I couldn't see my overalls, but I just assumed I'd get them when we got out. The cramped car headed towards Castlecary, a small village just off the A80 trunk road. Not a word was said to me during that journey, I could feel the stare from the angry faced man, directed towards me. When we got out at the job I realised the angry man had been sitting on my overalls. I never thought much of it, until I picked them up. They were soaking wet, and heavier than before. I later found out that Matt's old Ford Sierra had a leak. And the angry man thought it was acceptable to use "the laddie's" overalls to stop his arse getting wet. I suddenly realised that I had been afforded a very luxurious life while working one-to-one with Ally. I had maybe had life a little easier than some would've preferred.

That day on the Castlecary site I had a bit of a rude awakening. I had been used to Ally telling me, showing me, and then coaching me through what work I had to learn and complete. After pulling on my soaking overalls I received a mumbled instruction from Matt about first coating emulsion on ceilings, then left to get on with it. I was on a site of new build bungalows, still present today, and the atmosphere felt quite unwelcoming. Before, with Ally, he had a radio, a good wee system for working off the ground (an Irn-Bru crate which could easily be kicked around the floor), but this was essentially the first time I had worked alone. I was left with a 12" roller, pole, 10 litre bucket of emulsion, 3" brush, and a long wooden bench not dissimilar to those found in school gym halls- except this one was caked in plaster. The only way Matt helped was to make sure I thinned the emulsion down by the correct amount, and then he left. I struggled slowly, moving the bench around the perimeter of the room, cutting in the ceilings, and bringing the emulsion onto the wall slightly, just as Ally had shown me. The rooms were pretty small, and the bench awkward. I was getting frustrated at not having the same equipment as Ally had, therefore making me take much longer to complete the task. And before long, I realised that I was going to have to invest some of my next £45 wage in a radio of my own! I felt very lonely that day, the only people I encountered were other tradesmen coming in to work in the house periodically, and I never saw angry man the full day. When I had almost finished coating the ceilings, Matt arrived to see how I was getting on. He had emulsion spatter over his face so clearly he had been doing a bit himself. He mumbled that there was magnolia emulsion in a container out on the site that I was to use to coat the walls with. Then he was gone again. After sitting for my tea on my own for 20 minutes, I got back to work finishing my ceilings. Walking out to the metal freight container to get emulsion was very strange. I felt like a fish out of water. I was happy to return to the house and get on with painting; hopefully I would be back in my usual surroundings before long? If there's one attribute I have taken from that day it's that I learned not to get too comfortable in any given place or situation. The construction industry, whether you are a joiner, bricklayer, or any trade means that you follow where the work is. Whether you are working on a massive new build site with hundreds of houses, or a small loft conversion, there's only one certainty; the job will finish, and you will move on to the next one. Some jobs are great, some jobs are terrible. Usually this is mainly due to the location or the conditions. I used to love city jobs, places where there were plenty of people buzzing around. There was always plenty of distraction from the dull parts of the work. I can't say I "hated" any jobs but there were some which were less suitable than others. The Charing Cross job in Glasgow still ranks up among my most memorable, probably because it was my first one.

Ryan was settling in nicely at work. He and I both were. We had earned ourselves a decent reputation amongst the other workers as "good lads". We worked hard, and were keen to learn. We were both to sit a test at Falkirk College, an entrance test, for the Construction Industry Training Board. This was a government funded training initiative which part funded our apprenticeships. Having left school with four Highers, and thinking I was fairly bright, I hoped to pass alright. Ryan and I both did, and Davie later mentioned that the CITB officer had mentioned we passed at a level where we could have applied to be engineers. I still don't know if that was really said, or Davie playing mind games with his workforce, but we certainly took a ribbing off the tradesmen, which involved them trying to wind us up by calling us "golden balls", or "Davie's bitches", which we duly laughed off. The slaggings were good at that time, and most of the men were fairly sharp at it, and the best of it was they could take it back, but I was still very wary of going too far. The angry man, Joe, later turned out to be one of the sharpest witted men I have ever met on a site. He became quite a good friend through some of the tough times ahead.

That full summer was pretty enjoyable. We were working hard during the days with Ally mostly. One of the most amazing things about painting and decorating was that there were so many different skills to learn, and every day was different. One day I could be doing Aimes Taping, the next painting, the next day applying coving. There were so many different "mini-trades" within P&D that, I was actually amazed that anyone could be good at all of them! Ally continually impressed me with his skill. Having not done a particular task for some time, he could easily ,say, set up a ceiling for artexing, mark out a border, and apply two or three different designs in the artex mix on the ceiling -and get it right first time! I was learning loads of stuff from him. I was also learning a lot about life from everyone I met. Working on a building site wasn't easy, it took a very particular way of thinking to succeed, and fit in. Without being disrespectful, most of the labourers, tradesmen, and even site managers were not academic types. They were more vocational types. They were from mixed backgrounds, from places I had only heard of, but I had heard of them for all the wrong reasons. Places and areas of Glasgow like "Easterhouse" or "Shettleston" are still places I'm not at all familiar with, but I knew they were regarded as some of the toughest areas of the city. And Glasgow itself was generally regarded as one of the most dangerous cities in Britain, even Europe. Until recently, around 2010, it was the murder capital of Europe, only recently overtaken by somewhere in Ireland, "Limerick" apparently. So, at that time, in the mid-nineties, Glasgow was regarded as a pretty dangerous place, full of dangerous people... and I was working with its citizens on a daily basis

When the tradesmen came together at lunchtimes,

quite often in the howf, or site hut, or bothy, it could be amazingly wicked banter among them. As mentioned, these were mostly not academically clever men, but I witnessed some of the sharpest wits I have ever encountered on building sites. Some of the slaggings about the most menial of things were amazing. They would pit their wits against each other and do battle. Sitting around a lunch table, the discussions and slaggings could be about anything from the previous weeks football match to the new pair of overalls someone was sporting that particular day. Sometimes the slaggings would get a bit heated and there were plenty of times where I thought it were going to boil over into something physical, but it always seemed to stop just short. Every day was a new learning curve about something or other, and I was settling into building site life nicely. It was enjoyable! Different but enjoyable! Unfortunately, summer building site life was completely different from winter, and as the autumn came, college loomed and a whole new set of rules were about to be put in place.

College

We had received next to no correspondence from the college about our first day, apart from a date and time from Davie, so Ryan and I guessed what we would require for our first day. I must admit, it was a massive boost having Ryan by my side for starting college; he would've been beneficial to have been in place when starting work that day! I quizzed Ally as much as possible beforehand about college life; he went to the same one, though a few years ago. I asked about the lecturers, the buildings, the coursework and even the canteen. Pretty much all Ally could tell me was that I would encounter all the work that he did in college, and there were loads of girls there! Cheers Ally! I was particularly interested, in asking him about his "Apprentice of the Year" award, but he never really elaborated too much about it, only letting on that it was for his work in college. So, the weekend before we started I went out to town and bought a pen, pencil, ruler, A4 binder, and note pad. I packed a bag, and threw in my freshly washed overalls, along with a scraper and duster brush. After all, one of the first lessons I'd learned was "A good painter always has a scraper and duster on him".

Ryan and I had organised to get the bus together to Falkirk town and walk down to the college. Although I could drive, at this point I didn't have my own car, I only got to drive when my folks weren't using theirs. It was an eagerly awaited day, I had been looking forward to getting on with making my own way in this P&D world, and college was going to play a massive part in it. It was where I wanted to do well, and without being disrespectful, I hoped by having a few qualifications behind me, I may have the edge over my potential new classmates, as I estimated they may not be of the academic nature. But obviously, as Ally had shown me, being academically bright, was by no means any benefit on a building site.

That first day was another eye opener. When we arrived at college, we headed to the reception to ask where to go. We were directed down a corridor towards the P&D workshop. As we waited outside another few bewildered, nervous looking teenagers gathered. Every one of them looked like the "building site type" which I had become one of. Paint stained jeans, jumpers with splashes of paint, some even with the tell-tale paint stains on their hands. We were a scared looking bunch! Looking back, I can realise that for anyone, be it a kid aged five starting school, or an academic starting University, or *anyone* starting the first day in a new job, this is a very nerve wracking time. It's the fear of the unknown. What will the fellow employees, classmates, teacher, or bosses be like? Will there be anyone who will take an instant dislike to me? Will there be someone that could make life difficult for me?

All in all, I would bet that there are very few people reading this who have felt 100% comfortable in that situation?

As we waited, around 8.55am, a short, fairly rounded man came strolling around the corner. He was around mid-fifty's, with decreasing amounts of ginger-ish brown hair. He was wearing a pair of trousers and a "Sports jacket" type suit with collar and tie. As he walked towards the door, he glanced at us through his glasses and said "you's boys painters?" A few nods were his reply. He took out a bunch of keys and opened the door. I was about fourth to follow him through the door, and I walked into a wall of paint smell. It smelt like fifteen rooms had all been painted with different paints, and I was standing in a central corridor, where the smells gathered and mixed. I remember thinking to myself "what else were you expecting to smell, dick head?" We were ushered through a workshop, into a back room where there were lab style stools around metal covered benches. The benches were set out in a rectangular shape, and all the lads chose a position around them. I sat beside Ryan, not a word was being spoken as the man disappeared back out the door. As I had previously quizzed Ally about the lecturers I would get, I had a fair idea that the man who ushered us in was Geoff Jones. Geoff was a man from the neighbouring village to mine. I was told that he was a good guy, but that he wouldn't stand for any nonsense. I didn't know it that day, but Geoff would become a very good friend, a mentor, and would play a massive part in my career.

As we sat that morning Geoff came back with a bundle of forms, he took a seat a couple of people to my left. As we were walked through the process of enrolment forms, it became fairly clear that as I suspected, some of the students weren't of the academic nature. Again I have to make it clear that this was not being disrespectful, as I was fully aware hand skills did not require to be backed up with A-levels or Highers. But if I'm being honest, it did give me a slight boost. Here I was sat with a bag with folders, note pad, overalls and scraper, set for any eventuality- and some of the lads hadn't even bothered to bring a pen! This didn't sit too well with Mr. Jones, as I quickly realised he was to be referred to as, and he wasn't slow to lay into the offending students. After completing the forms Mr. Jones had a "wee chat" with us, where he clearly outlined that he would stand for no nonsense from any of us. He made a clear point of interrogating and intimidating us individually, asking which company we were from, and name dropping our bosses, just so as we knew that he knew them, and I got the impression he wouldn't think twice to contact them if we were anything other than good students. Message received loud and clear!

As for the other students, there were about fourteen in total. All shapes and sizes. Some of them were thoroughly forgettable, but some of them stood out. There was one boy with long hair. He was sat directly across from me. My first impression was that he was a rocker type. I was right. Stuart Millar became a close college mate to me over the next two years. Another lad who sat to my right was sturdily built and wore similar style clothes to me. He was another who became a close pal, Andrew Jackson. Most of the others were all to become pals, but mostly were forgotten and never really played any significant part other than banter and laughs. There were a few really funny boys in the class and some from some right rough areas. I never had anyone in the class that I didn't get on with; just I was closer to some than others. But to be fair, most of them would come into play with some wacky stories over the next two years! I wish I had kept better contact with those guys, but it was the days before mobile phones and social networking, but each and every one I had a great time with, and if I ever bump into them in a pub I will certainly buy them a pint!

During that first day, I never really spoke to any of the other boys, only Ryan. It was purely about induction and was very slow, intentionally I think. We went for lunch in the canteen, and spent the afternoon listening to the then C.I.T.B apprenticeship officer, outlining the instructions for site visits, work diaries, travel expenses, and on-site health and safety. I was pretty glad to get out after that day, but heading home on the bus I couldn't help wonder how much money Geoff Jones earned as a Lecturer. I was thinking to myself that may not be such a shabby job to have. Could this be a possible career me to aim for? Mmm, possibly! All in all, our first day of college had gone in fairly slowly. It was notably different to school, and also work, it kind of sat on its own in terms of being comparable to anything else. We were practical students, who sometimes did theory work, and attended college on block release basis. It was going to take a bit of getting used to, for sure.

Over the next six weeks of college I got to know most of my class mates fairly well. Apart from Ryan, I was closest to Stuart and Andrew. The two of them together weren't close at all but I got on well with each of them individually. I have found this to be a natural ability that comes instinctively to me. I dislike very few people. I'm very wary of a *lot* of people, but that doesn't mean I don't *like* them. I always think in the majority of people I can find something, be it a trait or mannerism that pleases me and therefore makes me like them. There has been the odd person that I have encountered in my life that I just don't like from the offset, but I can honestly say, I could *easily* count those on one hand. I got on well with Stuart; he was quite an outspoken, opinionated type of lad, with an interest in rock music, guitars and long hair. Andrew was the polar opposite; trendy, into to going to nightclubs and dance music. I got on equally well with both. I'm not sure if this is because I was kind of in the middle of their spectrums and could appreciate both of their interests and backgrounds. I knew I liked both of them, but in different ways. A massive part of liking someone, be it a man or a woman, is that if they can make me laugh then they are well on their way to gaining my appreciation and respect. Both of these guys were very able to do that.

Some of the other students in the class were lost in the first six week block of college. Some fell beside the wayside due to pay-off, lack of work, mis-conduct, or plain and simple not being any good at painting. There was always this constant reminder from Mr. Jones that if we didn't keep on our toes then we could be next. This was a stark warning that I always kept in my mind. I really enjoyed college life as an apprentice Painter and Decorator. Some of my classmates hated it, but I enjoyed the banter, the buzz around the college, seeing and meeting new faces. The days sometimes dragged in a bit, but that was part of college life, we would work for a bit, and then sit down for a while until others caught up. This made the day pretty tiring, something which I couldn't understand initially. I would work much harder out on site, but would be less tired after a shift. I guess the stop-start nature of college took it out of me. After a couple of weeks though, I realised that college life was fairly laid back, plenty of tea breaks, and some good banter with the lecturers. One of the lessons I learned from them was that if I was ok with them, they'd be ok with me; A life lesson I would take with me forever.

The P&D staff at Falkirk College consisted of four men. Geoff Jones was the Head of Department. Alongside him in full-time employment was Joe Lark, and there were two part-time lecturers, Larry Hatters and Albert Thomson.

Joe was a man of around fifty at the time. A slim built man. Joe had apparently been a Head of Department at another college and had taken early retirement, but decided further down the line that a return to college life was required. Joe was a fairly laid back guy, who also took no shit, but he clearly knew his stuff. He was very knowledgeable about paint, and everything to do with it. He had a very artistic edge; some of the work he could produce was amazing. He was the resident expert on marbling and graining. He used to gather us around while he worked on refurbishing a table or piece of furniture, it was amazing to watch. He would mix up stuff from little bottles and brush it on, wipe off, and produce excellent life-like timbers. He could do the most amazing things with paint. I often thought he was like a witch, mixing potions, and casting spells. He always had loads of tubs, jars, and bottles of wee potions that he mixed up. Joe would go on to play a massive part in my working life. He had quite a wicked sense of humour, loved a wee story, and a drink. It wasn't the first time I could smell the drink off him first thing in the morning in class. He by no means had a problem, just, like many Painters I know, liked a wee drink to relax at night. Joe was a really nice guy, quick witted, and sharp as a tack when he needed to be. He was very much one of the boys around the other staff, but was held in high regard, and commanded respect from others. During my college years, he was to be known as Mr. Lark, only later did I ever dare call him Joe. Geoff and Joe made a good team. They were close. They would cover for each other whenever one of them needed a morning off to conduct "a bit of business". They had obviously worked together a long time, respected each other, and knew where they stood with one another. Geoff dealt more with the "bread and butter" P&D, and allowed Joe to share what he was best at. But both guys clearly knew what they were about, clearly knew what they were teaching, and had obviously been doing it a while.

The other part of the team was made up of two part-time lecturers. They both had their own businesses outside of college, and came in for one or two days per week. Albert Thomson was probably the eldest of the whole team. He was a tall, moustached man. He had a strict attitude to work, almost like he didn't have much time for *any* teenagers, even the nicer ones. When we had him his nickname soon became "Captain Thomson". This was because when we were standing in the corridor waiting for class to start he would walk, in a very regimented manner, down the corridor towards us. His "battle cry", while still twenty feet away from the door, was "ENTER THE WORKSHOP, AND OVERALLS ON!" Again, I liked Mr. Thomson, there was something about him that made me respect him. He used to claim that he never believed in rollers for painting, as he could leave a much better finish, and do it quicker, with simply brushing. He claimed he was brought up before rollers were invented, and could brush emulsion onto a ceiling quicker than anyone could roll it. On hearing this, most of the class laughed and totally dismissed this, some even tried to tempt him into a money bet. But he was like an old sea dog, had probably seen all us young pups many times before, and never bit at the bait. Either that or it was all just bravado, in order to wind us up. Mr. Thomson was more of a serious type of guy; he rarely let his guard slip. If there was a hint of anyone trying to wind him up, he would boom an order at the offenders; his loud voice was enough to dismantle the uprising. I always felt that Mr. Thomson would've benefitted more, if he was to get to know us better, he always kept the line in place, and no one crossed it. The closest I ever got to him was one day out of the blue, just before morning break, he asked me to go to the canteen and get him a scone and butter, which I duly did. The scone arrived to him, fresh out of the oven, still warm, wrapped in a napkin, with a plastic knife, butter and jam. None of which he had asked for. For this I took a massive ribbing from the rest of the class. "Captain's bitch", and "teacher's pet" being some of the main put-downs I had to endure. But from that moment on, it became a ritual. Every day we had him, he'd shout me five minutes before break to go get his scone. He would shout "McKenzie!", and the other lads would follow it up with "scone time!" or "fetch my scone" in high pitched voices. It actually made me laugh along with them, as there was no harm meant by it. All in the name of good banter! Plus, from my point of view, it meant I got an extra ten minutes of break, and a walk around the college. But from then on in, we had a mutual respect for one another. I wasn't cheeky to him, and went for his scone, and he never got nasty with me.

The final member of the team was Larry Hatters, but Mr. Hatters while at college. Larry was by far the most laid back member of the team. Larry also used to teach one or two days per week, having a successful business running on the outside. Larry went on to become a very good friend and mentor, and still is to this day. He had a very likeable attitude about him, and he took time to get to know each and every one of the students. His attitude was very much that if the work was being completed on time, to standard, then he wanted to enjoy himself and have a few laughs with us. When I say that Mr. Thomson never let his guard slip, Larry always let his slip! If we were having a work lull, he would entertain us with stories from his younger days in Kelso, where he grew up. By all accounts he was a wild one, I loved hearing his stories, and they were fuelled with girls, drink, some drugs, and cars. He was a rugby player and a bit of a lad in his heyday. We would sit around chatting with him, sharing experiences, and he loved hearing any of ours that we could share. He gained massive respect from the students and only once had to raise his voice. Looking back he befriended us first, let us see that we were all on the same team, and then taught us how to paint. This was a very astute method of classroom control, but not something everyone could pull off. Everyone in the class agreed that he was their favourite lecturer, purely because of his manner, and I have to admit, he was the one I most looked up to. Others were possibly more skilful, like Joe Lark, others were more managerial, like Geoff Jones, but Larry had a manner about him which relaxed a learner, and made the work and learning, more fun and less boring. I didn't realise at the time, but watching these guys perform in the workshop was going to be one of the most important aspects of my apprenticeship. I enjoyed college, and working with the Lecturers.

Having had six weeks at college, I was looking forward to seeing the Glasgow job having progressed a long way. I was eager to show all the newly learned knowledge. I felt I had done well during those six weeks. When we returned to work autumn seemed all but over. I got a sharp warning of what was to lie ahead the first day back. I was taken as usual to the job on Charing Cross. On the way Davie explained to us that we were being shifted to Matt, his business partner's squad. The reason was that most of the work in Glasgow was done, and it only required a skeleton squad to finish it off. So Ryan and I were being shifted to another job, and away from Ally. Naturally, I was pretty disappointed as I saw Ally as the best source of quality learning I could receive from the company. Plus, my first taste of Matt's squad was not that of a favourable one. That day in Glasgow was pretty sad. I was surprised at the progress of the job. The block of flats was looking amazing! It actually looked like a really cool building. Most of the internal flats were completed, leaving only two stairwells to complete.

The scaffold had been removed and the exterior ground works were well on their way to being completed. There was nice landscaping at the back car park area, and the entrance vestibule looked really stylish. The full day I was gutted to be leaving the job. It had been a big job, my first job, and a part of me was sad to see it finishing, which was strange. It would seem that as a Painter and Decorator, I should've been glad to see it finished or nearly there, but I was left with a tinge of sadness that I wasn't going to be there at the very end. I was going to miss some of the other tradesmen and labourers from the site, most of whom had moved on while I was at college. It felt weird, like the end of an era, I would even miss the wee Asian guy who worked in the shop up the street! As I jumped into the van that night I felt less excitement about going to a new job, but more disappointment to be leaving that one. But, as I was to get accustomed to, jobs get finished and people move on. Some of those people I was to never meet again.

The next morning I was picked up by Matt in his clapped out Sierra. I was surprised the old wreck was still on the road! But as I waited for him to arrive, a man was waiting around twenty yards down the road. He had a bag and that familiar "building site" look about him. He looked like he was waiting to get picked up by another works van too. Matt pulled up and immediately rolled down the window and shouted to me "What ye's doing? Come on!!" I didn't understand. Ryan was already in the back, so I jumped in beside him. Matt pulled away slowly then stopped again twenty yards on. It turns out the other man was also an employee with the company. Obviously Matt must've thought that we knew each other already and were taking the piss by standing twenty yards apart on the roadside. I had never met him, or seen him before, but this turned out to be Callum, Matt's equivalent to Ally. He was sniggering as he got in, but Matt wasn't happy. Obviously if someone had told me there'd be another guy there I would've stood with him! And I'm sure he'd have done the same. This was an early sign of the communication break downs which would lie ahead in the future. We made the stop at the shop at Banknock and "angry man" jumped in. "Angry man" was not a suitable name for Joe Sneddon at all. He was anything but, but just looked that way. He gave off a fierce growl, but once his trust was gained he was actually very sound. He looked after number one at all times, but was a nice guy along with it. I was to get to know him well over the next few weeks. It was now October, and the mornings were no longer sunny. The air was cold, and the afternoons were darker. That first day at the new job was to give me a jolt.

We arrived at a housing estate somewhere in Cumbernauld. The job was a fire damaged house in a council estate. The car parked up and we all got out. Matt hurried us with our stuff into the house. It was dark inside with trail lights pinned to the walls to illuminate the rooms. There was rubble, debris, and waste lying over the floors in every area we passed through. Joe led us to the howf. It was cold and damp. I suddenly thought to myself how cold it had got since yesterday?! I suddenly clicked that the heating was now on in the flats in Glasgow, I hadn't even noticed, and because I had been in college for six weeks I hadn't really noticed the change in temperature. It was cold as I pulled my overalls on. I kept my jumper on under my overalls, clearly tomorrow I was going to have to be better dressed! Already I was feeling a dislike to this job, it was nothing like Glasgow. It smelled of burnt everything. Burnt, damp, cold, and dark. Straight away Matt was on his knees mixing up paint. He was pouring water into buckets of emulsion to thin it down, and stirring it with a stick. He handed me a bucket and one of the worst hand brushes I had ever seen. The bristle in it was all splayed out and the ferrule (metal casing) was caked in thick, dry paint. As he spoke to me I could see the breath coming from his lips. Brrrrrr, I thought.

I was instructed to paint out an upstairs bedroom walk in cupboard. It was heavily smoke damaged. That is, I finally got to see it was heavily smoke damaged once the sun finally hit the room. The darker mornings and absence of wired electric had meant that the house was powered by an external generator. From this, a series of cable lights, with bulbs every two metres were used to light the rooms. These were a complete pain in the arse, as the bulbs constantly blew, and the cables never reached where they were required to. They always cast shadows everywhere, and I constantly tripped over the cables. Every winter time job I've been on in my whole life which used trail lights, never had enough of them, never had long enough ones, or the ones they had were in terrible condition. As an apprentice, I grew to absolutely hate them! It was usually the apprentice's first job of the day and last job at night. Putting them out and plugging them in, and unplugging them, rolling them up and putting them away. The worst times were when it was a muddy building site, the cables had been lying in mud all day, and I would have to wrap them around my bent elbow and hand to roll them up. I always ended up soaking and muddy. Again, this was a problem which was only evident in winter. I was beginning to realise from my first day in Cumbernauld that winter time and summer time were to very different places in the construction industry.

That evening I had made sure I looked out some other old clothes to wear the next day. It was weird because I found it hard to choose clothes for painting in. I was in the situation I only had clothing that I wore. It was hard to choose which jumpers or jeans were closest to the end of their life span and consign them to the graveyard of "painting clothes". Being worn to work for one day would mean they could never re-appear as civilian clothes again. Guaranteed they would be marked in some way on the first day. So, I eventually picked out an extra t-shirt and two pairs of socks for the next day. Painting is a pretty physical job, a good sweat can be built up, but it's while your body gets to that stage that you feel the cold. Or there are some jobs that a person just never heats up while doing- painting railings or timber fencing. The next morning I was feeling wrapped up with two pairs of socks in my boots, and two t-shirts under a thicker jumper. I decided it was time to demote one of my trusted jackets to the "paint cemetery". When we arrived at the job I had a sense of feeling that nothing interesting was going to happen that day. I was put with Joe Sneddon to undercoat woodwork. We were supposed to abrade it all first then start undercoating it. Joe being Joe, he decided that *I* would rub it all down with the sandpaper, while he started applying paint to it. "Great", I thought, a full house of skirting's, facings, doors and window cills to sand. This would take a while. I had done plenty of rubbing down before, both in and out of college, to the point where my fingertips bled, but doing it in such depressing conditions was not cheering me up. The state of the house was unreal. Because it was a single house job, there was no outside container for storage, so all the other trades' equipment had to be stored in the house. That meant bags of plaster, timber, plumbing gear, all had to be kept in the rooms, usually piled against a wall that we had to paint, or a cupboard we had to coat. So this meant that every time we moved into another room to paint, the stuff had to be re-arranged in a manner which suited the task in hand. Paint the ceilings- move the stuff to the perimeter, paint the walls or skirting's- move the stuff back to the middle of the room, so as to leave the perimeter clear. It was a nightmare, and it was always the apprentice's nightmare!

As we had four weeks of work before we were back at college, I hoped we would get this job out of the road by the time we went, with a hope of heading to somewhere nicer when we returned. It was a long dark cold, damp four weeks. I would say that on that job I learned more about life than I did about painting. Although I was still very new to the job, I had a basic grasp on most of the work we would cover throughout the job, although I was slower than the tradesmen. I was working with Matt's band of men. Joe Sneddon, Callum Walker and Davie Mullen. I was also to have my eyes opened about Davie and Matt's relationship. As mostly the two teams worked separately, I was beginning to realise that Davie must be skimming the better jobs for his team, leaving Matt and his team with the less favourable jobs.

When working day-to-day with Joe as my tradesman, I learned that he was totally different from Ally. He could be just as skillful as Ally, but only when it suited him. Joe was what I would call, "fly". He was perfectly able to do a full packed shift of work, but on some occasions, chose not to. He was very aware that the company would not take the best of him. He liked to complete the work which was expected of him, and spend the rest of the day skiving. He would do no more than was required. If he was expected to get two rooms emulsioned that day, then that's what would be done, not a bit more. Working with him was funny, but could be a long day, as quite often much of it was spent standing around. Joe was the master of knowing where the boss was, when he'd left the site, and how long he expected him to be away. He would always find a room on a job where he could spy on people; keep an eye on what was going on. On a site of flats or houses, he was in his element. He would go into a particular house he was working in, place a small piece of timber leaned against the front door, and sit down (preferably with a newspaper). He used the carefully placed piece of timber, to act as a booby trap, if anyone was snooping about trying to catch him not working, when they opened the door the timber would fall over giving him an early warning so that he could get up and resume working before they got to the room he was in. Genius! I never once saw him caught. Before he sat down, he would always strategically place a paint brush or whatever tool was using, in place so he could react and grab it to assume work position. It took a few days of working with Joe, or Sneks, as he was to become known, before I gained his trust. Sneks, was a wary guy, never trusted many people, and was suspicious minded. But once I gained his trust we could have a laugh, and share stories. Sneks was good at storytelling, he was a funny guy, and I really liked him. I wasn't completely assured by his work ethic, but I put my trust in him. He was some man, everyone who worked there knew what he did, Davie and Matt probably did as well, but the thing about Sneks was he could deliver when requested. In days since then I would arrive onto a job which he was already on, and the first words he would tell me was the lowdown on who were "company men" or "grasses" amongst the tradesmen, and also if there were any pretty women who stayed opposite or close to the job! He was a handy man to have on your side, and I certainly wouldn't have liked to come up against him. His wing man was Callum, they played football together, and were close buddies.

Callum stayed around two streets away from my mum's house, in the area where I grew up as a kid. Callum was about the same age as Ally, around 23. Callum was built similarly to me, fairly small, slim, dark hair. I was very unsure of Callum when I first met him. He had just returned from his honeymoon, and the first meeting we had that morning when he stood twenty yards along the road waiting on Matt was a strange introduction. Callum was pretty short, and he seemed to crave respect, rather than command it. With Callum, everyone was an enemy until such times as they did something to make them a friend. I like to think opposite, everyone's a friend until they do something which makes them an enemy. Callum, whether or not due to his height, had a slight case of the "small man syndrome". I had this opinion as sometimes I had seen him walking around the site with his chest puffed out. It was almost like a peacock showing its feathers before a fight. Callum didn't drink, or seem to have much of a social life. He was newly married, had a nice house and nice car, obviously he was doing well, but I always got the feeling he had jumped into the whole marriage, house, possessions stuff too early in life and never took time to enjoy himself. Fair play to him though, he was settled down with his wife. I never really worked for long periods of time with Callum, and never really got to know him that well, but there was one day in particular that I got a good measure of what his ethos was about.

Sneks, Ryan and I were standing talking at the upstairs bedroom window in the Cumbernauld job. We were having a skive as we sometimes did with Sneks. Unusually, both Ryan and I were working with Sneks, caulking the woodwork in the upstairs of the house. Callum came upstairs and joined in the conversation.

Ryan, who was tall but very skinny, was getting wound up by Callum. I think Callum called him "specky", completely out of the blue, and Ryan didn't like it. Ryan replied by insulting Callum about his height, which in my opinion may have been his "Achilles heel". Tension heightened and I felt myself stepping back, in case it kicked off. The reason I was stepping back to let it happen was, Sneks was doing a bit of stirring the situation up. He was throwing in an odd comment to wind both perspective opponents up, hoping he would see some sort of humiliation. I watched intensely. I could see Callum was obviously perturbed by what Ryan had retaliated with, and not wanting to be shown up by a first year apprentice, in front of another apprentice and a fellow tradesman, he was going to have to flare his feathers in order to save face. This, I presumed, was a battle Callum had faced many times in life. I was thinking that possibly at school, he may have had some bullying issues. Callum, firstly tried to retaliate with some other kind of put-down, but with Sneks standing at the side winding him up, there had to be a stand-off. While Sneks was winding both up, both were diving for the bait. Although there was no real hatred or malice in the air it seemed more like a power struggle, and the seasoned tradesman was struggling to put the apprentice in his place. As the stand-off progressed, Callum and Ryan ended up squaring up to each other, with Callum looking up at Ryan. Callum had to make the first move to save face, and did. He grabbed Ryan round the neck, trying to put him into a headlock, but Ryan was too tall, they struggled bent over at knee height, with Sneks and me standing back laughing and cheering. They were almost locking each other's heads at the same time, struggling to win the battle for leverage, in order to floor their opponent. The battle may have only lasted a few seconds, with Ryan's superior height giving him the edge. He managed to twist the now red-faced Callum around and grapple him to the floor, to Callum's obvious surprise and disgust. Both of them had bright red faces, struggling and rolling on the floor, trying to get on top of the other. Ryan was getting an obvious advantage, and Callum was going to have to go some way to avoid a humiliating defeat which would follow him at work for a long time! And he did! In a last gasp effort to replenish some dignity and self-respect, Callum reached around with his right hand and gripped Ryan by the balls, and he didn't go lightly, he looked like a person struggling to get a lid off a jam jar. Ryan squealed and immediately let go in submission. Callum had saved face in the battle but in my opinion, Callum lost a bit of respect that day, both from Ryan and Sneks, but he got off lightly compared to what it could've been. I liked Callum, because he was good at his job. He may not have become a good friend like some of the others, but I respected him and his opinions.

Matt was quite a strange man in himself. His squad re-assured me that he was ok, but I never got to know him at all. He gave very little away. His relationship with Davie was very weird. Davie and his squad had the best of everything when it came to tools and materials. Matt and his squad were like the poor relations. Davie seemed to bully Matt awfully, even resorting to slagging him off in front of the men, and even us apprentices. I was told at one point that Matt was the junior partner, and Davie was the real boss. Matt had apparently made some glaring errors in the past which had cost the company money. It was purely the men's word I was taking, but according to them he and his men had fully re-decorated a woman's living room. It had been stripped, prepared, painted and cross-lined. It was over a week's work for two men. Matt had went in to hang the finish paper, and had somehow managed to hang an entire livingroom worth of paper, probably about ten rolls, of a value of two thousand pounds, upside down! I was told the woman returned to find flowers on the wall growing towards the floor. He had apparently not realised even then! Davie had gone berserk; he had the full cost of refund for the paper then the labour hours to cover. Another of the major mess ups from Matt happened when Davie was on holiday. They were painting a factory somewhere, and the specification instructed that the paint must be fire retardant paint. Now, fire retardant paint is issued with a certificate, if too much is bought it cannot be used on another job, because the certificate depicts where it has to be used. Matt, in his wisdom, decided to have normal emulsion paint mixed up, to the same colour, and instructed his men to apply it. This was a cost cutting exercise, as the fire retardant paint, as you can imagine, is very expensive. Emulsion is relatively cheap, and there was a massive cost saving. Unfortunately for Matt, there was a clerk of works on the job who demanded to see the certification, which Matt didn't have. This also apparently cost the company vast amounts of money and also a fine for negligence. Davie happily banded these stories about, even to us, and Matt was often ridiculed by Davie. Sometimes I felt sorry for him. But sometimes I could totally understand Davie's frustrations in him. There was only one time that I ever worked alone with Matt. We were doing an outside works one summer. He would leave me to get on with it all day. He would say very little as we ate our sandwiches in the sierra at tea-time. He was nose deep in a Daily Record. He always had a wee sleep at lunch, but set an annoying alarm on his watch so he would never sleep past 1 o'clock. There was one day I asked about his family. It turned out he had a daughter around my age, and he let slip that she worked in one of our local nightclub's. Ryan and I quickly spread it around work that we were going there that coming weekend, and we'd be on the lookout for her. Matt was fuming, but we didn't care. We actually did go there one weekend and spoke to her, and also let her know who we were, just so she'd let her dad know we had done it. Maybe put a wee bit of fear up him! The men at work loved it, they egged us on to try and ask her out on a date. I think for them, the thought of one of us turning up at his door to pick his daughter up, would be too much for many of them to handle!

Most of the time the two separate squads worked separately, almost like two different companies. Matt had to stop in at Davie's house every day after dropping the men off to give him the lowdown on what had taken place that day. Davie's attitude to Matt was that he was inferior, almost like he owned him. But I never once saw Matt stand up to Davie. When Davie was shouting at him over some sort of dithering, or miss-hap, Matt would just put his head down and carry on with whatever he was doing at the time, as if it wasn't actually happening. I was beginning to realise there was more to Davie than met the eye. At first my impression of him was of a successful businessman, a business owner who encouraged people to work hard for him. I was now beginning to see he was a bully, who didn't command respect from people, but ruled with fear and threats. Also, another thing I realised was that at any time, if he could get away with it, a few corners would be cut to maximise profit. Once when we were getting 10 litre tubs of emulsion poured into roller trays, he came with a bucket of water, and almost drowned us as he dumped the water into the emulsion mix. By the time I had it stirred together I wasn't sure whether to paint it on the walls, or wash my brush out in it! His words were "I call this pouring in the profit, son. Pour in the profit!" Obviously, the more he thinned the paint the larger area it would cover; therefore the less he would have to buy. I was learning, not all good learning, but I was learning a lot. Someone once said to me "you can learn as much from a poor tradesman, as the knowledge you gain from a good one." I was finding this true. But soon enough, and quite gladly, I would be heading back to the warm comforts of the college.

Back to College

The first day back at college was a bit of a relief. We were back for four weeks. Hopefully four weeks of relaxed learning, looking at girls, and being in out of the cold. The weather was taking a turn for the worse, it was November after all. We were instructed that we were starting a scaffolding unit, which was going to be partly completed outside. I was gutted at the thought of having to go back outside to work in the cold, but at least I'd be prepared for it. There was another couple of "victims" who had not appeared back. One in particular, Harry Kirkby, had apparently left his company. We were all very intrigued as to why this had happened, as Harry was a good laugh. He was a daft kid, and not the brightest. He was quite often the butt of jokes. He was a chubby lad, who had a big impression of himself, but his impression never quite matched up to others'. He would often come out with ludicrous stories, which I think he expected the rest of the class to believe. And more often than not, he would find the worst possible timing for the worst possible remarks. It was safe to say, that in six weeks of college, he was the clear front runner for "figure of fun." Even Larry Hatters had started slagging him off a bit, but in a joking way. We all liked him, and missed him when he wasn't there, as he kept us going with his daft stories about far-fetched sexual conquests, and weekend battles which he always won, and prevailed totally unscathed from. Even Geoff Jones didn't know what had happened to him. It was in the days before mobile phones became popular, so nobody had his contact number to find out. Harry was a constant source of amusement. One time in particular, early in the course, were being instructed on how to gloss a window frame, and the method and procedure for completing it the best and easiest way. We had Larry Hatters this particular afternoon. Larry was the most laid back, and as long as the work was getting done, he didn't mind the smokers slipping out the back to the bricklayers store to have a fly smoke. Harry must have been pestering Mr.Hatters for a quick smoke break, but we were instructed that if we had finished our window, then people could go for a fly fag. Most of the people were fairly well on with the window, but Harry was one of the slower workers. Looking up, I saw Harry disappear out the back door. I was thinking he must've got a real move on with his window?! A few minutes later while still painting my window frame, I heard Stuart in a fit of laughter coming from an adjacent cubicle. I walked over to investigate. There Stuart was, tears streaming down his face, buckled over nearly in half, laughing aloud. He was pointing at Harry's window. In his nicotine starved haste, he had slapped *loads* of gloss on as quickly as he could so he could get out back for a cigarette. He had misjudged how much gloss could run if not spread properly, which, clearly, he hadn't taken time to do. The gloss was dripping off the window cill onto puddles on the floor. As we watched in amazement, word spread to the whole class, who soon gathered round. Still Larry didn't have to raise his voice. But he did make Harry come in from his fag break and scrape the excess gloss from every part of the window, re-brush it so it could dry, then scrape the paint off the floor, and eventually clean with rags and white spirit. He had to stay in the workshop over break time to clear it up. The next time we had Larry for painting he went through the normal process of instructing us on the work to be done and the standards required. He issued the full class with the normal gloss, then from the back pulled out a tin of non-drip gloss and said "here Harry, you can use the special-needs paint!" We were all howling with laughter at this. This was exactly the kind of stuff we loved him for; he kept us laughing at the dull times. As we got on with our work that first day back, everyone felt a little sadness that Harry Kirkby was gone.

The love interest?

Over the next four weeks we had all sorts of work at college. We were progressing well, and getting to know each other well. The Lecturer's became a little less strict, as they could see we weren't a threat to anyone. We were a decent bunch of lads. And for a while we became a decent bunch of lads, and a girl. The second day back we had a new start to the class- a girl. She came down the corridor with Mr. Jones, she was quite pretty, wore quite a lot of make-up, and *didn't* have the "building site look". Her name was Jenny, and as soon as Mr. Jones introduced her, and explained she had just been taken on as a P&D Apprentice, and joining our group due to the severity of our reduction in numbers, I could see everyone drooling over her. She had which seemed to be an oversized chest for such a petite body, and I couldn't resist a quick look myself. As we went into the workshop, and as usual got shifted into our overalls, Jenny was taken by Mr.Jones and issued a new pair. Immediately, all the boys were winking at each other and passing under-breath remarks and smirks about having a girl in the group. This was a fairly closely knit group of guys, and all I could think of was how she would integrate into the group? And where would she be working? All the guys were clambering over each other to offer to work beside Jenny. She was six weeks of college behind, and would clearly need some sort of support to find her feet, and get her settled in. After briefing us on our work for the morning, Mr.Jones brought Jenny down to the cubicle adjacent to mine. The one vacated by the much missed Harry Kirkby. "Harry who?" I thought as he told her this was where she was going to be working. "Will you keep an eye on Jenny, Jimmy?" "Yes Mr.Jones, I'll certainly do that!" Jenny had been issued a pair of boiler suit style overalls. The only problem being that, her chest was so big that she couldn't button them all the way up, so there was quite a view on show. I introduced myself and explained what we were doing. Jenny seemed to be nice. We chatted away about nothing in particular as the morning progressed. It was nice to have a scent of perfume in the workshop for a change, rather than the stink of paint and turps. The only problem was her cleavage was so eye catching, that it was difficult to look at her face while speaking to her! As the morning slipped closer to break time I realised that I had never had so many visits to my cubicle by the other lads to talk about nothing in particular! The testosterone was buzzing around the place! When we approached break, again, the boys were clambering over each other, wetting and re-shaping their hair, spraying deodorant, and offering to show Jenny where the canteen was. It was hilarious to watch.

The day went in fairly quickly, and I enjoyed getting a wee chat with someone new, especially a girl, during class. We left that evening and said good bye to everyone. Ryan and I were laughing to each other about how funny it had been, and how desperate some of the lads had made themselves look, all of the way home. It was certainly going to provide more laughter, we agreed, as sooner rather than later, someone would ask her on a date, and the possible outcomes could be hilarious. I was really enjoying college, and doing well, I felt as if I was probably one of the better painters in the class. I certainly believed I had shown I was in the top half, and I got on well with all the staff. I was looking forward to getting on, and progressing well, as

I wanted to have my name on the winner's board up high in the workshop, which I had my eye on from day one. There had been about twenty names on it from the previous years, I wasn't exactly sure what it was for, because I hadn't seen Ally's name on it. On asking Mr.Jones about it, he said it was a prize board for winners of a defunct competition. Well, that's what I wanted to aspire to anyway.

The next morning we were still laughing about how ridiculous some of the lads had made themselves look, slavering over Jenny. I thought to myself, if I was single, which I wasn't at the time, I certainly wouldn't want a girlfriend who was a painter the same as me! I could imagine her working on building sites, and if it lasted, doing homers with her. Na, not for me I thought. It didn't matter anyway, because when we got in to the workshop there was no sign of her. When class started and she hadn't turned up, the lads all started blaming each other for "coming on" too heavy and scaring her off! We later found out from Mr.Jones that she had received the offer off a job as a secretary, and had accepted it, which was something she was probably more suited to. We never saw jenny again! And the workshop was back to stinking of paint and turps once more...

Travelling back and forth to college on the bus was a bit of a pain in the arse, because we had to walk to and from the bus station in the town centre, which was a twenty minute walk. So, I was really glad when my big sister got a new car and gave me hers. I was newly turned eighteen, had my own car, and generally thought I was quite the "boy about town". Ryan had offered to give me half his travel expenses towards my petrol, so we both were a bit better off while still claiming bus travel expenses. It was still a pain as all the other lads had to walk to the station so I would still drop some of them off before going home. Here I was, eighteen, own car, and still only earning £45 per week as a first year apprentice. I certainly never had much left to splurge on alcohol, now that I was drinking legally. In fact, at that time, I wasn't really into drinking. Through the week, after work I would just hang about with my mates in cars, or I would see my then girlfriend.

While on that block at college the class had knitted together better still. We were a close bunch. We used to go for a pint the odd day at lunchtime. One lad, Stuart, used to put the same song on the jukebox at lunchtime when we went to the pub. "Come on Eileen" by Dexy's Midnight Runners was his song of choice. A strange choice as it was from the 70's, but we all grew to love it, and hummed and sang it all afternoon, after returning to the workshop with a "one pint glow". I wasn't a big fan of having one pint at lunch, as I always got a mini-hangover in the afternoon. I still do to this day, a couple hours later I just have a headache, and feel de-hydrated. Some of the younger lads didn't go, as they were still 16 or 17, but the majority did, but not every day. We never had any bother from the staff about that, but I think by that stage they just turned a blind eye, as we weren't causing any trouble. We would work away in our cubicles all afternoon, singing away. The lecturers must have either been jealous because they knew what we'd been up to, or if they didn't realise, they must have been a bit bewildered as to how our attitude had changed from before lunch. It was safe to say, with the state of Scottish winters, I was enjoying college life much more than I was on site. This was about to be confirmed, with one of the most memorable jobs I have been on in my whole life. I was about to learn the harsh reality of what life on a building site was *really* like.

The Rude Awakening

After the Christmas holidays I had a four week block at work. We were starting a new job, again in Cumbernauld. It was in an area called Carbrain, the area in which Cumbernauld train station lies. The job was to refurbish houses which had a garage on the ground floor below the living quarters on the first and second floors. In more affluent areas, they are generally known as Town Houses. The garages were to be converted into kitchens, and the rest of the houses refurbished. Cumbernauld is a "new town", built in the 60's to house people moving out from Glasgow. It had a bit of a bad reputation as a town, with its poorly designed dwellings, which probably looked good when the idea was first conceived. Carbrain, at that time, was one of the worst areas of Cumbernauld, and it certainly lived up to its reputation. We were to be there for the next four months, Matt and Davie's squads together, although probably not the whole time. The job had already begun, but it wasn't quite ready for us before Christmas. The first work to be done was to Aimes tape the new plasterboard put up by the joiners. Ryan and I were both sent straight away with Sneks and Callum Walker. I presumed we would be doing the taping and any other basic stuff like priming new wood, but I was in for a shock. The first morning we arrived on site, I felt total sadness. The site was mucky, with big mounds of excavation work taking place around the buildings. There was only a site hut, a canteen, and a toilet. The houses had been ripped apart, right back to their bare shells. The temperature was really low, probably about -2°C. As we went to where we were to begin work, my disappointment was difficult to hide. Coming from two weeks off during Christmas, back to work for a long drive to Easter was bad enough, but coming to this site, along with the weather, was breaking my heart. I kept telling myself "Just keep thinking of the work".

Keeping myself thinking positive about the potential learning and experience I could gain from this job lasted about twenty minutes! It was freezing cold. The room we arrived in to get our overalls on was stinking of dampness. I dumped my bag down and pulled my overalls on. I suddenly realised I had nowhere near enough clothing on. This was going to be a VERY cold day. Matt was briefing Joe and Callum on what houses were to be started first. When he arrived back in the room from showing them he had two buckets and two large wall brushes. As he handed us them he instructed us that we were to scour the first block and soak and scrape any wallpaper which remained in the houses. We weren't getting steam strippers, we were just to wet the paper and scrape it. I knew we would be at this for a while, and in the current temperatures it would be gruelling having wet hands all day. The only saving grace was that we would be doing it together. We started in the house we were in. It was cold, and dark. The only light we had was from the 110 volt trail lights, the ones I had grown to hate, the ones which never quite reached the room you needed to work in, the ones that never had enough bulbs and what they did have were constantly blowing. As usual, the cables were extended from a transformer out front, and lead into individual houses. They were a complete pain in the arse, but it was the only light we had in the mornings and late afternoons. In January and February, there's basically only a maximum of three hours of good sunlight, less on a cloudy day. These lights were essential to get work done, but I hated them with every bone in my body! We managed to get freezing cold water in our buckets from the site stand pipe. As we started with the large eight inch wall brushes or "slushers" as they were known, I began to realise what a miserable day this was going to be. We worked together in a room at a time. Firstly ripping off the top layer of paper, and soaking the backing paper, which could then be scraped when soft. It was laborious work. When I reached up to soak a high part, the freezing water would run down my arm. After only a few minutes, I could feel my hands numbing up. My wrists were already sore with the weight of the slusher. My heart was sinking, and the only lift in mood I could get was from Ryan. I just hoped he could step up to the task and somehow lift my spirits.

This was an employment all time low for me. I was in a damp, dark, freezing house in Cumbernauld. It was the first Monday morning after the Christmas holidays. I was wet and cold. I didn't even have a radio to listen to as the batteries in mine were low and it was struggling to get a signal. I truly hated this! I knew I certainly didn't want to do this for the rest of my life. As I stopped for a second I looked at Ryan scraping furiously at paper. The thoughts of self-doubt were creeping in. Had I made a mistake in becoming a Painter and Decorator? Was I deluded with summer painting and working with Ally? Was this what life was going to be like? It was truly gruelling, and it was for £45 per week. As I re-joined Ryan with the scraping, I was mentally working out how much I was earning that day. It wasn't difficult- £9 per day! Suddenly I was filled with despair. I was being put through this for £9 per day! I felt angry at that thought. Angry at Matt for making me do this. Angry at Davie for not telling me it would be like this. Angry at Ally for not being here with me. Angry at Ryan for not telling me a fucking joke or story to cheer me up... but most of all, angry at myself. I was angry because I had thrown away all the hard work I did at school; I may as well have ripped up my Highers certificate. I had thrown away a place at University to be paid £9 per day for basic slave labour. Work that I'm positive a monkey could be trained to do! Maybe I had made a mistake? Maybe I had another chance to change my mind? Maybe I could make a U-turn? Maybe I was stuck with this for the rest of my life.

I tortured myself that whole day. And the work tortured me more. The only break I got was to go to the shop for the men at lunchtime, and then join them to cower round a Calor gas fire for a half hour lunch break, making myself feel ill with the fumes just trying to get a heat in me. By the time the afternoon came, I was glad to see those damn trail lights being switched on again, as I knew if it was getting dark I'd be going home in a little while. How the space of eight hours had changed my opinion of those lights! I was never gladder to use them. As 4.30 pm approached, I had all but given up the will to go on. For the last half hour of the day Ryan and I skived, Sneks style! I put the lessons he had taught me into practice and placed a "booby trap" at the back of the front door. My early warning system of an old piece of skirting placed against the back of the closed front door. That would be enough to let us know if Davie or Matt, or anyone was coming to visit us. It was that time of day when a lot of workers on a site would finish up what they were working on and have a wee quiet time, or skive, as long as they were out of sight from bosses. It was the perfect time for me to quiz Ryan, ask him what he thought about this kind of work, ask him if he thought it was for him, and hopefully find some solace in his answers. He was pretty unrepentant about his day. He wasn't keen on the work, or the conditions, and certainly not what we were being paid. But he said something about it, probably the one thing that made me go back again the next day, the only thing; "Jimmy, we're the bottom of the pile, the apprentices, we're gonna get shit to do for a while. And we're gonna be paid shit for doing it, but we're kinda paying for the training we're receiving." I thought about that all the way home in the van that day. He was right. We were doing manual work, hard work, and there wasn't a lot of learning getting done; but in a way we were paying for our college training. That was the one and only reason I was standing waiting to be picked up that next morning. That evening I got showered and warm. I watched telly the full evening and warmed myself at the fire. I also looked out more socks, gloves, and tracksuit bottoms for under my jeans. If I was to stick this out I would have to keep warm.

That Tuesday morning I woke at my usual time. My alarm seemed so much louder than normal. As I lay awake in my warm, comfy bed, I dreaded the thought of getting out and pulling on my stinking paint clothes, and plenty of them. As I sat having coffee and cereal, I pondered what may possibly lay ahead for that day. One thing for sure, after looking out the blinds, it was going to be as cold as Monday was. I stood as normal waiting for Matt. When we arrived at the site Matt had a special surprise for us. He asked "Do ye's want the good news or the bad news?" "The good news" Ryan blurted out. "Well, you're not stripping paper today" Excellent I thought, but what was the bad news? "but the bad news is, ye's are sanding in front of the tapers" Just as I thought things couldn't get any worse than yesterday; it did. The sanding was to be done with sanding poles. A sanding pole is basically a flat pad around 200mm x 75mm, to which is attached abrasive paper. The pad is attached to a pole with a swivel hinge, which allows the user to abrade walls and ceilings. It's very awkward, tiring work, especially on ceilings. The Aimes taped ceilings and wall areas were to be abraded with this, and hand sanders. Even nowadays, there's no modern, more advanced, or easier method of doing this, still the same old sanding pole and abrasive paper. It's the kind of job people hate, especially tradesmen, but if there was one thing I learned, it was easier to rub down some Tapers work than others. Aimes Taping could be mastered to the stage that there was very little rubbing required, but mostly a vigorous rub was required.

That morning we were to rub down the ceiling and walls which had been taped and filled the day before. As it wasn't the final sand it was only a light rub, but it gave us a taste of what we were in for. It was freezing temperatures again; we could see our breath as we twisted the wing nuts tight around the abrasive paper. We were working in the same house but would take a room each, one at a time until the house was rubbed down. I always started with the ceiling tapes – the most awkward part. If anyone has ever used a sanding pole on a ceiling, one of the risks is that if the pad slips, and the swivel hinge spins too fast, the pad can flip over gauging the wing nuts into the plasterboard ceiling. This was happening a lot to begin with that morning, and I was getting increasingly infuriated with it. As you can imagine, the sanding is almost always delegated to the apprentices. In some places I've worked the sanding pole was referred to as "the stupid stick", referring that no brains were required to work it. In general it was for use by people who were paid from the neck down. But, as apprentices, we became very proficient with them. The rubbing after the third coat of plaster was the most vigorous one; the walls had to be completely smooth and seamless. This work produced body heat, which in winter was good. But it never stopped a person's feet and hands getting cold. It was especially sore on the shoulders, and the dust which it created was horrendous. Because the ceilings above you were being sanded, the dust would fall directly on your face and shoulders. We were supposed to wear dust masks and goggles, but Davie and Matt rarely had any. Today an employer would go to jail for such sins. After sanding a full house a person resembled a snow man or a baker as the other trades guys used to say. The dust would gather in the corner of your eyes, making them dry and bloodshot, in your nose making it white and dry, and in your ears. It would be perfectly normal to be picking white gunge out of my ears, nose, and eyes for the full night after a day of sanding, with my eyes resembling that of a crazed bag snatcher. Goodness knows what it did and is doing to my health. I still have a residual, recurring ear infection in both ears; which was the result of working in a dusty atmosphere. It felt amazing to get home and have a shower after a day of it, but I never really felt properly clean afterwards, and my skin and hair always felt dry. The bloodshot eyes were an after effect which often resulted in conjunctivitis, which meant peeling scabby eyelids apart and picking out white gunge straight after waking in the mornings. All in all, the sanding was not good for a man's health, there was and still is so much risk to painters with lung problems due to the dust and fumes we encounter. As I said Davie often didn't have masks, so I always made sure when he did get them that I kept a couple of spare ones. Even the ones he did buy were the cheap disposable ones, which never fitted properly, and only protected a little. Once when I asked him for a mask he told me, in a rather condescending manner, "Son, you don't need a dust mask. I have asked my doctor about it, and he said all you need to do is have a wee drink of water to wash it down once you're finished". I actually felt insulted that he expected me to believe that! The dust was being breathed into the lungs, not the throat, but Davie must've thought that I was young and naïve enough to believe him.

Those days were the worst I have *ever* encountered. The winter of 1995 turned out to be one of the coldest in the last thirty years. At one point in Cumbernauld the temperature never went above -12°C for almost a week. It was horrendous. Combined with the darkness, and the freezing temperatures, it made on-site life absolutely gruelling. Everything was a struggle. There was no running water on site, as the pipes were frozen solid. The fork lift drivers had to shuttle in barrels of water from God knows where. Ryan and I were on sanding duty the whole time, probably for a month solid. The only break we got off it was either to go to the shop with an order to get the tradesmen stuff for lunch, or to wash out the tradesmen's rollers, having to break the ice on the water barrels, and plunge already cold hands into the freezing water. Sometimes it was good when one of the men came to hand us a roller, tray and brush to wash out, as it got us off sanding for a few minutes, but it was a painful task as afterwards my hands were aching in pain with the cold. This was, and still is, the grimmest time of my life. The only thing that kept us going through this period was the trusted radio; we would play "name that song" games, or sing, or guess the year, just to take our mind off the mind numbing work of sanding houses. The depression I used to feel on a Monday morning on that site, that winter, was something I have gladly, never come across again. The thought of the only breaks we had were fifteen minutes at 9.30 a.m. and half an hour at lunchtime. By now we were well tooled up with

"Thermos" flasks, thermal underwear, and more often than not, something hot to eat from the local shop. We would gather with the tradesmen in the howf for breaks, a room in a house not yet being worked on, some sitting on dust sheets, some on paint tins. We crowded around a "Calor" gas fire, in a bid to get some heat in us, but more often than not, only succeeding in making ourselves ill with the fumes from it. It was like something from pre-historic days. I couldn't help think we were like cavemen gathered round a fire, it reeked of desperation. I could barely move for the amount layers I was wearing, only peeling some off when I got warm from sanding, covered in dirty dust, freezing cold hands and feet, nose constantly running. My heart was broken whenever the first man got up to resume working. Starting again after a break was like starting first thing in the morning, except I now had a headache from the fumes from the fire. There seemed to be no let up. At times I felt like going to Matt and begging him to take me home. My hands hurt, my shoulders and arms hurt, my whole body was freezing cold, the work we were doing was shit, and we were doing it for £9 per day. This was tough! I had never felt so desperate in all my life. I felt totally low. There was nothing that could cheer me up, apart from maybe somebody or something happening to make us have to go home, and go home right now.

It was a complete relief when we jumped into the van at night and got the heater on. I was desperate to get home, get a shower, and some hot food inside me. I was dreaming of lying in front of my parents' fire, lapping up the heat as it hit me. The feeling when I actually got there did not disappoint. It was glorious, but I knew it was only a few short hours until I was right back out there. The days were excruciatingly long, and the evenings passed in a flash. Day after day, we kept at it, it got to the stage I began to hate my life. The doubt and resentment crept back in. I longed for college life again. There seemed to be nothing that I liked or enjoyed about this life. But, unfortunately for me, I was as stubborn as the days were long. I had to keep going. I had to get through this nightmare. I looked for something to pick my mood up every day, a laugh, a joke, a funny story, anything. Not very often, but sometimes I would get it.

One day after lunchtime break, the tapers had asked me to go and fill two large 20 litre buckets full of water from the water barrels. I was particularly low that day. I dunked the buckets one at a time into the barrels, my hands freezing instantly in the ice water. As I did this I thought to myself "Please God, please help me, please give me a sign that I am going to get through this. Please show me everything is going to be ok?" As I trudged slowly back along the scaffold to where the men were working, one of the joiner apprentices was working on the frozen ground below me. He had two joiners' benches around 1.5 Metres apart with a sheet of plywood balanced on them. This particular lad was well known for his lack of intelligence on site. Word had already swept round the site that he was a bit of a "victim" among his peers and tradesmen. He was nicknamed "The Butcher" because of his willingness to carve up wood. His weapon of choice on this occasion was a circular saw which he was about to wield. As I trudged slowly back, my arms straining to carry the buckets in each hand, bouncing off my knees and splashing freezing water over my boots, I watched him, wondering what his next move was. He had obviously marked a line to cut up the middle of the sheet. As he kneeled on the plywood sheet with one knee, he lined the saw up to his line and pulled the protection guard back. The sound ripped from the saw as it began to chew threw the wood, but unknown to "the Butcher" his full body weight was leaning on the middle of the plywood sheet. The saw, uncontrolled, ripped up a waving line, in about 2 seconds got to two thirds of the width of the timber, where his body weight took over, snapping the remainder of uncut wood into a ripped, splintered break, the lad still holding the spinning saw crashed to the ground on top of the pile. I nearly dropped my buckets. Straight away a roar of laughter came from all working close by. Shouts of "haw you ya stupid cunt!" and "fuckin' hell butcher!" rung across the site. It was simple, but it was funny. People were falling about laughing at the lad's misuse of equipment. I've always thought there's something hilarious about someone *nearly* seriously injuring themselves. It was enough to tell me the "Big Man Upstairs" was listening. On telling Ryan and the men the story I got a little lift for the rest of the day. It was just enough to lift my spirits for a bit.

There were a few really good laughs on that job, but they were well outnumbered by the bad parts, but in fairness that was partly down to the horrific weather and conditions. I had never seen anything like it, and the only time I have since, was the winter of 2010/11, but luckily I wasn't working on site. The laughs at the time were very important to me; it was what kept me going. One of my duties as a first year apprentice was going to the shop for the men. While on the Glasgow job I had recognised a famous person, Rik Mayall, a famous comedian from T.V. He had done shows like "The Young Ones" and "Bottom". I had passed him while heading to the shop. I later found out he was in Glasgow with his "Bottom Live" show at the time. I was with Ryan at the time and he didn't know who he was which kind of ruined the moment to be honest! Going to the shop for the men was a laborious task, collecting orders, money, going and getting the stuff, dealing with the change etc. But, this was all time away from working, so it felt like an extended break to me. At the Cumbernauld job, this was a little bit more of a chore. No matter what time I visited the shop there always seemed to be at least one person drinking Buckfast standing outside, even at half nine on a Monday morning. And they always seemed to have at least one large killer dog beside them. I had heard stories of joiner apprentices being hassled for money from them, with the area having a high proportion of junkies, people were always vulnerable if they were suspected of carrying an amount of money. I always made sure that I had some sort of sharp tool in my scraper pocket in my overalls, my preferred weapons being a putty knife or a pair of paper hanging shears. I thought to myself, if anybody starts on me, they'll get this in their neck! But on the many occasions I had to walk by them, they never really bothered me. Although it didn't stop me feeling a bit intimidated at the time. I was the "shop boy" for the painters, and "the Butcher" was my counterpart for the joiners. I'm no too sure I was happy to be likened to him, but I always thought to myself that no matter what, I was getting the better end of the bargain. Also, it was possible to skin a couple of pounds each day which went towards my lunch, whenever I didn't bring sandwiches. I always used to write down the order on a scrap piece of paper or a small bit of timber. I remember queuing behind the Butcher one day in the shop. He had in his hand a small piece of plasterboard drywall. On it he had written his tradesmen's orders. When he had been served and left the shop, I was next being served. The woman looked up at me and said "See that boy? Every day he comes in here wi' a bit o' plasterboard. Av got enough here tae build a hoose!" It seems the Butcher had left his piece with her on the counter everyday. She picked it up, looked at it and said "look, he actually wrote doon he wanted a packet o' smookey becoon. Is that meant to say smokey bacon?!" I laughed to myself at his spelling. Bless him, but was far from the brightest!

A Star Among Us

Getting through the worst winter in years was a massive boost for me. It couldn't surely be as bad as that again next year? And anyway, if it was, I'd make sure I was better prepared for it. As the harsh weather passed, things got a little easier. The work became more enjoyable, and I started to see some progress on the job. And the breakthrough day for me, was the one where I saw the first part of bright sunshine. I was not long after lunchtime, one day in February, I was painting all the front doors of a row of the flats. As I felt the sun hit down on my back and neck I removed my woolly hat for a minute, stopped painting, turned round and looked up at it. "Where have you been all my life, you big bastard?" It was a sign that winter was on its way out, and spring was coming. "Thank Fuck!" I thought to myself, almost saying it out loud. It was probably around this time I became aware of everyone talking about a guy who was working on the job. A guy with the surname of "Buchanan". Everywhere I was on the job people kept mentioning this guy's name. The more I heard it, the more I wondered what it was about and who this guy was. Eventually I asked why everyone was talking about him. I was told his name was Ken Buchanan. "Who?" I thought to myself. Being eighteen, thinking only about football, girls, and alcohol, I had no idea who Ken Buchanan was.

It turned out Ken Buchanan was a Scottish Undisputed World Champion Lightweight Boxer. I had no real interest in boxing, let alone boxers from the past. But, as it turned out Ken Buchanan was and still is, a legend in boxing. He famously held the world lightweight title in the early 70's and lost it in a famous defeat from Roberto Duran, from Panama, at Madison Square Gardens, New York, a defeat which should never have happened apparently. At the end of the 13th round, with Buchanan ahead on all three score cards, he took, what his trainer claimed was, a knee to the groin. This rendered him unable to fight, and he lost his title. I was amazed by this. I set about finding out more about him, and I wanted to meet him. He was working on the job as a joiner. The first thing that came to mind was why on earth would someone who had been as successful as him need to work in a shit hole like this? If he was as successful as I heard, surely that glory would come with some riches? And if I was him I certainly wouldn't be working in that hole as a hobby! I asked my Dad and a couple of other folk about Ken, and I was informed that he had lost a fortune due to poor business decisions, and misguidance by his bank. He had apparently returned to his job as a joiner/carpenter to pay bills and get by. I did eventually meet him on the site. I remember walking into a room in a flat one day to begin applying emulsion. Davie was already there, speaking to a man. This often happened; Davie spent a large portion of his day standing talking to people, when he was supposed to be working. As I worked I listened in to what was being said, and to my joy I heard them talk about boxing! That must be him! As I worked, now and then I turned around to get a glimpse of him. He was a slim man, not much taller than me, around 5'10", with short greying hair and glasses, and the usual building site appearance. Davie had obviously been asking him about his past as he was in full flow of what seemed like a "well used" story. At one point talking about the Duran fight he began bobbing and weaving around Davie, who, to be honest, looked like he was going to shit himself! Ken had quite an aggressive manner about him as he talked, and he still looked like a very fit man, so I reminded myself not to get on his wrong side. He had an interesting vibe from him, and I would've loved to sit down with him for a chat. By this point, Davie looked nervous as Ken was getting a bit carried away with the story, bounding about an empty living room, tool belt still around his waist, re-living that famous night. I think he was glad to get out of there for fear of receiving a mis-guided jab. I never really spoke to Ken, as at the time he wasn't on the job for very long, probably a two or three weeks. After that first encounter, I saw him around the site, held a door open for him a couple of times and said hiya. Word spread soon that he was leaving. He had apparently been offered some training job in the United States. He had been inducted into The Boxing Hall of Fame, and was apparently more famous there than he was in Scotland. So, one Friday, he handed his apprentice every tool he owned and left the job for good to head off to the States. I later heard that his dream job hadn't worked out as well as hoped and within a couple of months he was back in Scotland, back to being a joiner. He must've been gutted. I didn't know him well, but I felt for the guy. It seemed like he had lived the ultimate dream, and as far as I know, had it all taken from him.

Years later, when I was browsing a bookshop, I came across his autobiography. I instantly picked it up and bought it. On reading it, after the main part of his career, he actually mentioned that job in Cumbernauld, for Lamont Builders, where he had taken a call that offered him his training job in the States. He told how he gave up his tools and headed off for a better life, back to the sport he loved, and for it all to end up a disappointment. I was amazed, star struck a little, that someone so famous had been through exactly the same as I had on that job. And I couldn't help think "Damn it, if I had only got to know him better I might've got a mention in his book!" I never saw Ken Buchanan again, but I'll never forget meeting The Undisputed World Champion, that doesn't happen to many people, especially not a wee Painter from Denny.

The Prodigal Son Returns

After the depressing slave labour of the freezing cold Cumbernauld site, I was only too happy to return to college for the first of our remaining two-week blocks. It felt like I was going on a two week holiday when I jumped out the van that Friday afternoon. I had reached rock bottom on that job, mostly due to the weather, but also just how the job was. I prayed that I'd be sent somewhere else when we returned. I had what I could only describe as some sort of depression. I wasn't actually ill, but so fed up with work that it made it feel like I was. As soon as 4.30pm came I was totally fine again, for a few hours at least. That morning when we walked backed into the college, I had never been gladder to be wearing only one layer of clothing, a *clean* layer, and a jacket. The temperature felt nice in the college as we walked through the doors. As we approached the Painting corridor, I noticed a figure leaning against the wall. A strange face. As we got closer I could see, low and behold, it was Harry Kirkby! Harry, having previously vanished from the course without trace was back! He had been missed when he was away, he was a fun figure to have around, and always kept the conversation going, always making us laugh with his antics. But where had he been?

As we got talking, Ryan jumped in with the question on both our minds. Harry went on to explain that, when we left college that time, he went to work with his boss. It was a small company, just Harry and his boss working together. They had been working in a large Manse in Stirling. The whole house was being redecorated, but this particular Wednesday morning

Harry's boss had left Harry to go and collect some materials. In the large living room there was a "Sash and Case Bay Window", a large three part curved wooden framed window opened with pulley strings. Harry's employer had quickly briefed him on the work to be done while he was gone. Briefly he was instructed to sand the window, the facings, skirtings, and doors, all in preparation for him coming back to help Harry undercoat them. Well, as Harry explained, being relatively new to the job, and not having a visual description, only verbal instruction, on what he had to do, Harry armed himself with a coarse graded abrasive paper and started rubbing the glass pane of the window! He spent forty five minutes alone rubbing the glass panes! When this was complete, he began working on the timber frame, at which point his boss returned. On walking into the room, his gaffer spotted the rather frosted looking appearance on the glass. On closer inspection, he went absolutely berserk at Harry, sacking him on the spot! By this point a few of the other guys in the class had gathered and were listening in to Harry, we all roared with laughter, uncontrollably roared, to the stage Harry's face went scarlet. I could not believe what I was hearing? Apparently, Harry went on, he had caused over two thousand pounds worth of damage! This was the reason he had never appeared back when meant to. Once we had all calmed down, he later explained that as part of his contract, the then C.I.T.B training Officer, was obliged to find him alternative employment with another company. This guy was bullet proof, I thought to myself. How could he be so naive to think he was to sand and prepare the glass part of the window?! It beggared belief. But sure enough, it seemed to be true. I was, frankly, amazed! But, for all his sins, it was good to have Harry back, and he settled in again with no problems. I wasn't so sure, however, that Geoff, Joe, and Larry were so happy to see him back, but the story sure as hell must have gave them a laugh at tea-time.

Those two weeks at college passed fairly swiftly and easily. The work was enjoyable, and more importantly, I was learning again. I was enjoying watching the lecturers and learning as much as I could from them. They were a very interesting, and intriguing bunch. They had brilliant, funny stories, about jobs they had done, places they had been and experiences they had. Some of them we heard more than once, but I just put that down to the years of breathing in paint fumes! Clearly this had burnt away some vital brain cells, which resulted in them not remembering telling us a particular story. I didn't mind because if the story got further fetched the second time, it was a good indication it wasn't actually true. But, with Geoff, Joe, Larry, and Albert, they all stayed the same the second time. I was learning as much about other things as I was about painting. Stories about owning a business, working abroad, and working in college intrigued me no end, and it was making me more interested in getting into lecturing eventually. I tried, in vain, to ask how much money these guys earned as lecturers, but they weren't for giving up any information. I tried to watch their teaching styles as much as possible. Geoff's was a pretty straight laced teaching style. "Bread and butter" learning. Joe could afford to be a little more flamboyant, as his artistic skills, and the work he created, tended to hold our attention more. Albert was very regimented, shouted quite a lot, but him and I had an understanding with his scones! Larry was like a mate, totally on our side, and he made us want to work for him, he was so laid back, could make us laugh, and his stories were brilliant. Quite often, if we had worked hard all morning, he would sit with us in a cubicle, and just talk. This could go on most of the afternoon, with very little actual work getting done. Larry was great though, it wasn't all about him, he was just as keen to listen to our stories, and he loved hearing about my depressing days on the Cumbernauld job. He was keen to listen to, and get to know all the lads, and as far as I know every lad liked him for it. And as soon as he gave the word we were back to work, keen to get on. For me, this was a direct contrast to say, Matt mumbling a set of instructions, then disappearing. It's probably pretty lucky that it wasn't Ryan or I who had sanded a window pane, Harry Kirkby style, with the way he mumbled his instructions. I kept thinking, how enjoyable it must be for the people who worked for Larry. He must've been a good boss to work for. And it was also making me realise a few flaws in Davie and Matt. I never heard Larry raise his voice once, up until one particular day.

As we were all getting along very well, and respecting each other, Larry used to let us sit in the workshop over break time. He would be away for about twenty minutes at a time for his tea. We would normally just sit with juice and have a chat, or wind each other up. But this particular day, the group was a bit livelier than normal. For some reason, possibly a full moon or something, but they were hyped. Someone had noticed there was a loft hatch in the workshop ceiling. Somebody decided it would be a great idea to have a look up in the loft space to see what was there. Ryan and Andrew were keen to get up there, and as there was an abundance of step ladders in the workshop, access was easy. As the boys shifted aside the hatch, and climbed up, I watched almost giggling like a school girl. When they disappeared, we could hear them going some distance. They were back within a minute proclaiming that it was possible to walk all the way along and look down into another classroom! Unfortunately, they had to walk along a timber joist which the ceiling was attached to. Immediately, I remembered a film I had seen years ago, "Porkies" in which a bunch of high school kids had done the same, and had a peep hole into the women's shower block. I never went up but I'm pretty sure it wasn't like that. The only problem that occurred during this school boy prank happened on the way back. The two guys were laughing so hard, that Ryan slipped off the joist and his foot crashed through the ceiling. We all heard the noise and straight after it the noise of something landing further down the workshop on the floor. Andrew came to the loft hatch, trying to get down as rapidly as possible, laughing hard, and trying his best to explain what had happened. Next was Ryan. As he climbed down the step ladder, his chalk white face had clearly had a fright. Someone ran down the workshop to find a whole about 200mm^2 in the ceiling of *my* cubicle! We were all laughing hysterically, that is all except Ryan and Andrew.

The next ten minutes were spent trying to hastily concoct some sort of feasible explanation as to how this damage may have occurred. It wasn't easy, as the blow which broke through the ceiling had clearly come from above. This was clearly damage which had not happened from the ground. In the end, the best we could all come up with was that Andrew had accidentally thrown Ryan's lighter through the hatch and when he went up he slipped off the joist and through the ceiling! Nobody thought of the fact that he damage occurred about twenty feet away from the hatch! It wasn't exactly a water tight, fool proof plan, which would result in us all being commended for bravery. But, it was all we had, and we (they) had to go with it. It was at this point that the lads who weren't involved, started to distance themselves and hurriedly find something to do as to look busy when Larry got back. I decided to busy myself with stripping some wall paper which we had been doing that day. As the door swung open, everyone's heads were deep in work. I think he knew straight away something was amiss. As he walked around the workshop, everyone beavering away, there was a bemused look on his face. He sensed the atmosphere as if he could smell the guilt. As he got down to my cubicle I was nearly shitting myself. I had never heard Larry getting angry, but I knew I didn't want to. Although he was a great guy, I still knew I didn't want to be on his bad side, and I reckon if he needed to, he could handle himself well. As he came into my cubicle, the gaping hole was almost above his head. Although he may not instinctively look up at it, the pile of dust and debris on the floor under it was a bit of a giveaway. Sure enough, as he walked in, his eye was drawn to the pile, instinctively followed by a tilt of the head to look up. He paused for a second; I could almost feel his brain working through the process like a crime scene investigator. He would surely fathom it out that it was caused from above in no time... And that he did. "Right, either one of you wee bastards have been up in that loft space, or this workshop has suffered an attack from the I.R.A.!" He wasn't happy. That was the first time I had ever heard him shouting. He glared at me for an explanation. As I wasn't in the situation where I was keen to grass on my peers, the only movement I could offer was a defensive shrug of my shoulders. He must've realised that it hadn't been me, and quickly walked around the other cubicles, hunting down the guilty party. Larry had the nose of a beagle when hunting for guilt ridden pranksters. He quickly picked out Andrew and Ryan, partly due to the fact that Ryan's face had switched from being ghostly white, to the red shade rather like that of a hardened drinker. He brought them both into my cubicle and pointed at the ceiling. I could do nothing but keep working at the stripping. With my back to them, Larry was sharp with his word and his tone. Ryan and Andrew were feebly mumbling some sort of poorly concocted story about the cigarette lighter, each of them contradicting one another at almost every opportunity. It was pretty embarrassing for the both of them. I glanced round at one point to see Larry's finger pointing at Ryan, while his head was closely examining his footwear. Andrew was looking at Larry, his face bright red. Larry Ripped through them both, left them red faced, but with the result that they were going to have to repair the damage themselves, and in their time. That would take care of the next few lunch breaks for that pair. The best part was that Larry offered to not let the other staff find out, so long as it was repaired correctly and swiftly. This was a major result for the lads, as Geoff Jones may not have had the same leniency with them. It could easily have been construed as a breach of health and safety, which could have ultimately ended in dismissal for the boys. A right result, by all accounts! Larry had proved, even in this situation, that he had the students best interests at heart. He could've easily had both of them sacked, right there and then.

Larry was very rarely heard shouting again. The only other time I heard him raise his voice was when Andrew placed a 5 litre tin of gloss paint on a shelf in the paint store. The problem being he never placed it *fully* on the shelf, and I watched it fall, in slow motion, to the ground, where the lid burst open, and the full 5 litres of paint spilt and splashed over the place. It happened fifteen minutes before the end of the day, and we were kept back late to clean it up. We used a full bag of rags, and around four litres of white spirit to clean it up. Andrew was slagged about that for ages, people missed buses, and were not amused. The next day though, everyone could see the funny side. That was generally the college year over.

It was around this time that my mate Chris, who also attended Falkirk College, got me with a belter of a practical joke. He was studying Graphic Design at the college, and therefore had plenty of art materials to hand. One afternoon, while I was busy working away in my class, he excused himself from his class and went to find my car in the car park. After locating my Mk 1 Ford Fiesta, he made a template of the rear number plate. When I left college at my usual time of 4.30pm I jumped into my car, drove home through Falkirk town centre, through Camelon to Denny, in nose-to-tail traffic for the majority of the journey. After dropping Ryan off at his house I headed home, where I parked up my car and headed into my folks' house, where I lay on the couch awaiting my mum coming home from work to make my tea.

As I lay, watching TV, when my mum arrived home she came in laughing. I was half asleep as she came in the living room and asked "Have you seen your car?" This confused my greatly as I had driven home in my car so obviously I had seen it!?

My mum led me out, laughing almost hysterically, to see my car. When I got there, it was the first thing I noticed...

On the back, there was a fake number plate, made from card, painted yellow like the real rear number plates are, and on it was lettered with realistic font...

PE N1S

As I saw the letters, the realisation suddenly started creeping in. Who had done this? How long has it been on there? Where have I been with this on?

"aw naw" I thought, it had to be Chris. It had to be him. He has access to the necessary materials and skills to do this. Aw naw!! I must've driven through Falkirk Town, and Camelon Main Street, in traffic, with this on! I could feel my face going red, I felt like someone had suddenly turned the heating up as I stood in our back yard. The bastard! I was laughing as well! I was *very* impressed with Chrissy's genius thinking, and also his 007 James Bond artwork, but I had been had, and I had been had in front of many, many people!

I had to put my hands up, and admit he got me good and proper. Well done mate, I think I *still* have to repay you for that day. It certainly gave me, my family, and the rest of our mates a good laugh.

As the year came to a close at June we had all passed our respective units and were looking forward to a summer on site. We had completed a lot of work in our first term at college. I was happy; I had endured the worst weather conditions of my life, and had come out the other side a stronger person, both physically and mentally. I knew there were still some nagging doubts about whether I had made the right decision to start in P&D, but I was comfortable that if I was to keep going I would have fewer surprises in the coming year than that of my first year. And I felt I had given a good account of myself. My attitude, work produced, and general demeanour, I felt I had shown that I was at least worth my salts as an employee. This summer and the next year were going to be important. I had been asking and showing a bit of interest in the Painting and Decorating competitions, in which each college were represented. I was keen to represent my college, I saw that as an amazing opportunity to shine, not only within the college surroundings, but it would give me some benefits at work as well. I looked forward to hopefully being involved! Plus, it would mean I was in 2nd year, which meant an increase in wages. My pay would go from £45 to £70 per week. How would I spend that extra money?! But with it, would come extra responsibility. Davie had already made that clear.

Summer Again

That summer on site was back to being enjoyable. We were working with Davie and Ally, in another part of Cumbernauld, near Broadwood stadium. It was a new site of new-build houses and flats. Ryan and I were back to taping with Ally, back to good work, back to P&D being cool, and back to working hard and feeling happy again. I was enjoying the work again, and Davie was starting to catch on that I was capable of much more than just manual graft. He was giving me extra responsibility of driving the van to pick up materials, measuring house interiors for his pricing/estimating purposes, and he was letting me tape houses on my own. This was good for me as he trusted me to work alone, and with other stuff. This was probably lucky because while scrambling up a roof to paint a chimney on an exterior work, Ally fell off the roof and damaged his knee, meaning he was going to be off for at least six weeks. This meant that Ryan and I were Davie's top tapers, with the responsibility of finishing the site and the work until Ally returned.

During this period Ryan and I went up in Davie's estimation. He could've, and had the opportunity to, pull in guys like Callum and Joe from Matts squad, but he never. He knew we were good workers, responsible for our age, and more than capable of producing good work. At the time he had a nickname for us. He used to call us "his home-grown tomatoes", a term referring to the fact he was training us to the stage where he could use us in the company. This was a happy period, although we missed Ally, and Davie was pretty rough when he was on the tools, the work was good. The extra responsibility was good for us, but I had a feeling it wouldn't last for long. That full summer we worked away, taping houses, and eventually painting some of them, until Ally returned. In Davie's eyes, there was no one quite like Ally. Admittedly, I looked up to Ally. He was what I wanted to become. He was a good role model. He was good at his job, and he could do it in a way which looked effortless. Davie used to say that he was "the son I never had", he trusted him that much, and he proclaimed at times that he had written him into his will. Whether that was true or not, I don't know, but it showed how much he respected him. I wanted to be like Ally, he had an heir about him, was respected by others, and could make working hard look effortless. Having Ally back was good, it meant we could return to being the apprentices, with more of a focus on learning. That summer was a great learning curve for us; the responsibility would stand me in good stead for what was to come. We were rapidly becoming a viable and respected part of Davie's workforce, and I was enjoying having the respect from the men. The overall vibe while working with Davie and Matt was that the men were all pretty close. Deep down they considered Davie and Matt to be not only the bosses, but the enemy. They were a fairly close knit group, who had a decent level of trust among each other. This was partly due to Davie's wild outbursts at times. As mentioned, he almost bullied Matt, and if someone had let him down he wasn't shy to vent his anger, but he would do it in an undirected fashion. He would sit in the front of the van, driver's seat, and be cursing and shouting, but not at anyone in particular, because he never directed it at anyone personally. I think this was because he was afraid of direct confrontation. I had heard stories of a former employee, who had left to start his own company, any time Davie passed him in his van, Davie would flick "V" signs at him, and verbally abuse him out the window. But once, while buying paint at a local store, Davie returned to his van to find the man waiting for him. Apparently Davie went chalk white and couldn't get away quick enough when challenged. The story goes the man tried to square up to Davie but his reply was "why would you want to fight an old man, son?" To me, along with the thinly veiled van rants, I could see Davie had no real back bone; he would never challenge someone on what they had said or done directly. I had witnessed this a few times in the van, Davie upfront letting off outbursts of swearing, everyone would know who it was directed at, even the person on the receiving end, but mostly people just sat and tried to ignore it for fear of losing their job. I would soon encounter this myself, but the wee man was never one for backing down from a bully.

Davie's reputation as a bit of a nasty piece of work preceded him. Stories were aplenty about Davie. Some amazed me, some made me laugh, and some I felt a bit embarrassed for him. I also learned a lot about him that I never knew. For example, he was more of a business man than I thought. He used to own and operate one of the local chip shops, and he was the first in the area to own a video hire shop, back in the early eighties when VCR's came about. Apparently he never really did too well with anything other than the painting business, as he was still working in his early sixties, and still is to this day. He didn't seem to be a well-liked man, stories of him being forced out the local bowling club and "black-balled" from the local Masonic Lodge, showed that he wasn't really a people person. He didn't get on well with people. But he was easy to manipulate, a little ego massage and he would put a person in his good books.

2nd Year

After that summer we were firmly in Davie's good books. We were working hard and effectively at every area of P&D that we encountered. By this point Ryan and I had been trained in Taping, Coving, Artexing and Paperhanging as well as all the skills that were involved in normal painting. By the time we went back to college for 2nd year, I was almost wondering what else there was for us to learn? But going back to college, we would soon find out what was the motivation for the year ahead. At the end of the summer, before we returned to college, we were surprised to find that Davie had put our wages up. The 2nd year rate was £70 per week, what would I do with all that extra money?! When we returned to college on enrolment day, we were to find that most of the guys were back. If I remember correctly, there were a couple of guys who had decided over the summer that painting just wasn't for them, and had left to try ventures new. The class was getting rather bare, probably down to around nine or ten. We found out during induction that the main units we would be learning that term would be decorative skills and patterned and ceiling paperhanging. There was always some theory work thrown in, and the properties of surface coatings unit would be memorable but for all the wrong reasons.

"Properties of surface coatings" was, and still is, one of the driest, potentially mind numbing units. It basically is a topic about all the ingredients that make up a tin of pain. Talk of resins, binders, vehicles, and film formers was enough to send most students into a world of sleep battling. Not only that, but the unit was entirely theory based, with every session taught in a classroom setting. So, the first day we had the unit on our timetable I was one of the first students through the door and I plumped for a desk and chair near the front of the room. We had Geoff Jones for the unit and his first task was to hand out the photocopied workbooks. It seemed to be a fairly sizeable amount of paper which landed on the desk in front of me. Mr Jones then preceded to read through the introduction to the unit. To his credit, Mr Jones tried his best to make it sound appealing, but in a three hour session, listening to him talk about this stuff was making people fall asleep. As I looked around there were some students up the back slumped in their chair, and I myself had phases where I was having that old internal struggle to stay awake. I found myself doing the self harming nip of the inside leg, or pull a nostril hair move, to provide my body with enough pain as to snap myself out of the sleep deprived inner struggle. Mental note to self; next time we have this class, sit at the back! Thankfully, this was only a minor park of our course, which during induction would be fully outlined.

The main part of induction which stuck in my head was that of the competitions. It was explained to us that 2nd year was the first of the competition years. These competitions were basically inter-college competitions where the best students from each college were chosen to attend an event at a particular college centre, participate in producing a panelled competition piece, which encapsulated all the relevant skills which we had learned. They were usually a full day in length, and some were Scottish heats for the British, European, and even World finals. There were a few competitions going at that time which are slightly varied from these days. At the time there was "Crown Young Decorator of the Year", "Skillbuild", and the "S.A.P.C.T

Competition", which stood for the Scottish Association of Painting Craft Teachers. Nowadays there are more competitions, mostly sponsored by large paint companies like Dulux and Johnstone's. Within these competitions there was usually a craft section for 2nd year students, and an advanced craft level for 3rd year students. While in 2nd year it was customary to enlist for the craft division. I knew, on learning about the competitions, that I had to be involved in these. I had to be part of it, and more importantly, I wanted to win. I knew that if I wanted to be considered the best, then having a victory at one of these competitions under my belt was a must. Plus, if Ally had won an award at college, then I wanted to show him and Davie that I was as good. So, that was my target and goal set out for the year, and as we were only attending college for twelve weeks in 2nd year, I would have to get a move on. I had to make the most of learning everything I was taught, both at work and college, and firmly grasp it as I did.

As we were now into 2nd year and had been a good find for Davie, he decided to take on another new apprentice to follow behind us as a new 1st year. James was chosen in a fairly similar way to me, Davie knew his dad. James started around the time we returned to college, but when we met him it didn't take long for him to blend in. James was a quiet, likeable lad. He went about his work in a quiet manner, and I always got the impression he had been shy as a kid, it took quite a bit for him to come out his shell and let us get to know him, but eventually we did. Davie had obviously been encouraged by the success of Ryan and me that year, enough to venture into employing another one.

Our 2nd year went fairly normally, along the same path as our 1st year. The one main benefit was that I knew what to expect. When the days got colder I knew what to expect from the weather, and I was well prepared for it. That preparation didn't stop me praying for a less "lively" winter though, surely it couldn't be as bad as last year? We were moving from job to job, seeing a fair bit of the local country, never venturing too far from home. Some of the work was good, some not so good, but we took it as it came and always looked to Davie to let us know where we were to be heading next. Davie was getting fairly involved in the new build housing boom which began in the late nineties, and a major portion of his work evolved around this. It was at this time that we had a job in Gargunnock, a tiny village just north of Stirling. There was a street of new houses, all of which we were taping and painting, probably around twenty houses. We were only on the first two houses which were to become the "Showhouses" for the development, when one day near lunchtime a van pulled up. Out jumped half a dozen burly men, who began telling the workers to remove their tools from the side and leave immediately. What was going on? I didn't understand what was happening? The men were being very aggressive in their manner and their orders to leave all materials on the site and remove only personal tools was being carried out very swiftly. It turned out, the company who were the main contractors of the job had gone bust that morning, and all of their current jobs were being evacuated so that the firm's value and losses could be calculated. Obviously there would be people owed money, and that would have been dealt with in due time but the primary concern was getting their live sites closed down without people looting for tools, materials and equipment. As the news spread over the site, Davie was frantic. He was shouting to us all to gather the equipment into the van, his face had went a strange colour. Apparently, Davie had been waiting on a cheque for around six thousand pounds from the company for work we had done, he had asked a couple of times as to when he was getting paid, but never thought too much about it as the company always paid eventually. Not this time. As Davie had no other work at the moment because his full squad were on the job, we had no other option but to pack up the van and go home. The van was a sullen vehicle that day on the way home. We were all dropped off early to go home to explain to wives and families that our jobs were uncertain and explain what had happened. Davie reckoned that he lost around seven thousand pounds from the collapse of that contractor, a massive amount for any company, let alone a small business like his. None of us knew if we had a job to go to the next day. At the time Davie had no other work scheduled, as the job was a big one which required the concentration of all his men. It turned out after a couple of phone calls that evening that Matt was putting the word round that we were to take the rest of the week off, unpaid, until he and Davie could re-arrange some of the future work they had planned. The loss they suffered was a big enough amount to floor a lot of companies, but we were lucky Davie and Matt must've had enough in reserves to see us through more work paying for labour and materials until the next cheque came in.

Having a couple of days off to relax while Davie and Matt sorted things out was a God Send for me. Sure, I wasn't being paid, but I wasn't bothered. I lived with my folks, I had some money put aside, and I could comfortably live for a while off that. I had no responsibility, not like the other men who had families to feed and bills to pay. So, I relaxed, hit the gym, and generally did what I would if I had a weekend off. It felt like I was on holiday, wearing my good clothes, knowing I wasn't going to get covered in paint. While I was sitting one day, I realised though that I could've been out doing a homer (a private job on the side), and earning myself extra money. I wasn't too bothered, but decided then to make a start on beginning my career on homers. The way I saw it, it would benefit me in more than one way, I would get more money, and I could practice the areas of P&D which I didn't often get to do with Davie, like paperhanging for example. The kind of stuff I was shown and learned to do at college, but if not practised, those skills and techniques could be easily forgotten. I wanted to make sure that I not only remembered them, but I also wanted to enhance them by getting more proficient and quicker at the different disciplines. I was conscious that after my final year in my apprenticeship, I was to sit a "Skills Test". This was a two day test which incorporated all the disciplines in P&D, and one of the major test pieces was on paperhanging. I had begun to realise that not all painters seemed to do paperhanging. It was a skill which many did not feel comfortable doing. To me this seemed insane! Having a trade qualification, but being unable or unwilling to participate in a large part of it? It was only really Ally and Callum who hung paper along with Davie and Matt, the rest shied away from it, which, to me, seemed very strange. A lot of companies had men who only did paperhanging, and they were paid the top rate, more than anyone. It was also seen as being the cream of the work, clean work. I was keen to be good at *every* area of my trade, so I wanted to make sure that I improved my paperhanging skills I had learned at college. Doing homers was the perfect way to do this. So I started putting the word around that I was available for jobs, mainly small jobs, and it would be perfect to start with friends and family.

Starting Homers

I had already started buying some of my own tools. At work, we used Davie's tools. He had a van full of everything we needed, and enough brushes for all of us. But I had started buying tools for myself, in order to eventually start homers. The first jobs I did were for family, which I did for free, or next to free. Then I began to get work from mate's parents and friends of friends. These were ones where I could charge a little more while still staying safely in the realm of "mate's rates". I only really did the work at the weekends, with the odd evening thrown in if required. Looking back, I had a massive confidence about my ability at that time. I'm not sure if it was because I was young, but being very inexperienced, and taking on some pretty big jobs, I didn't have any fear of messing up, and potentially costing the customer a fortune. I suppose I was driven by the confidence I had gained on-site, and also at college. I was warned that it may be slightly too early to start homers, but I didn't listen. And looking back, I was pretty lucky nothing went wrong. I never made any mistakes which cost me or the client, and the jobs always got done effectively with a quality finish. So, the more jobs I did, the more tools I bought, therefore meaning the more jobs I could do. I never really asked to borrow any tools from work, I didn't like to. I'd been warned that borrowing tools from Davie resulted in a situation where I would owe him a favour, and he would take that as an admission to be willing to work a weekend or late whenever he requested. Plus, I wasn't keen for him to know how much I was doing, not that he minded, but I just thought he might use it against me if I accidently over slept one morning. Maybe I was being cynical and a bit harsh on Davie, but that's just how I felt at the time. He didn't need to know. It was while doing my homers that I began to think that it may be a possibility to start up in business myself. This is a consideration I have had many times now, and still to this day I consider it. Especially when I'm fed up at work! So, as the jobs came in and the jobs were completed, the wallet got a little fuller, as did my dad's garage. I was getting to the stage where I had tools to complete most tasks. Paperhanging, Taping and Filling, all painting, even Artexing, were all skills which I had the relevant tools to complete. I would work away on a homer at weekends, not making that much money, but it was good practice and experience, and the people were loving a bit of discounted decorating! Everything was going perfectly. Word was spreading, and the phone was starting to ring often. Word of mouth was my only advertising, and I went on positive praise passed on in the hairdressers or supermarket from Mrs. Jones on finding out Mrs. Smith needed a decorator. One of my pals' parents had passed my number to a friend, and I went to see her about the work.

This particular job was a living room. A new partition wall had been put up, that needed taped, with the ornate coving to be matched in, the full existing paper stripped, and the entire living room cross-lined, ceiling and cove painted, top paper above the dado rail, and a striped paper below it. I had worked a couple of evenings through the week, as it suited the small taping work required. When I finished the taping, coving and painting, I was onto the lining. The job was fairly big in terms of what I normally attacked, but the woman understood I was only going to be mainly working at weekends, and she was fine with that. By the time I got to the finish papers it was a Saturday morning, and I had my eye on having the full job complete that weekend. I worked all day completing the top paper and the majority of the bottom. This left only the remaining bottom part and a border which was to go around the full room. There were two radiators in the room, one of which I had removed, drained, applied the paper neatly around the brackets, and replaced successfully. The other was still to do. I decided to go back on Sunday morning, with a view to being finished in two hours and being paid then. I had a pre-arranged night out on the Saturday night. All was well that night; I had a good few drinks but kept myself relatively in check, knowing that I had a bit of work the next morning. Having got in pretty late, I set my alarm for 9 am. I arranged with the lady to let her have a long lie, seeing as it was Sunday, and it would help me after being out. So I woke up at 9am and still felt a bit drunk! After a coffee and a bit of breakfast I set off for the job. I was still pretty worse for wear by the time I arrived, but thought it'd only be an hour or two before I was done. So, I set about papering up to the second radiator. I set about removing and draining the radiator, finished the paper behind it around the brackets, and along to the corner. I decided to replace the radiator before commencing with the border. I placed the radiator back on the brackets and started tightening the valves back on at each side. One was tightened successfully, and there were no leaks when I checked. While tightening the other side, I kept checking with a piece of tissue paper, and there kept being a small leak. So, I tightened it a little further… still leaking. So, I tightened it another bit…. *Still* leaking. I went to tighten it a little more….**SNAP!** The micro-bore pipe going into the under-side of the valve kinked in the joint and started spraying roasting hot water all over me! To say I got a fright was a bit of an understatement! I grabbed a dust sheet and muffled the spray with it, not knowing what to do? My initial reaction was to tighten further, but that made the kink, and the spray, worse. I was soaking wet by this point. The woman was upstairs, and I realised I couldn't hide this disaster. I shouted for her to come down, which she promptly did. I asked if she knew where her water turn off switch was. Eventually I found it, turned it off, but there was still water in the system which had to be drained. Not knowing much about the system I didn't know where that drain off point was?? By the time I found it, the entire heating system had drained itself onto her living room carpet. There was a massive circle of jet black, stinking water on her carpet, so black that it hid the pattern on the carpet. The woman was in surprisingly good spirits. By this point I was a wreck. I kept thinking that I was dreaming that this disaster wasn't actually happening. But it was. Every part of it. It was five days before Christmas, and I had just wrecked this woman's living room. She insisted that her brother in law was a plumber, but he couldn't come until the next day. She phoned her daughter as well. She arrived round very quickly, and was rather less amused than the woman. I explained that I had done it a hundred times before, and never once had any problem. She told me in no uncertain terms that I wasn't a plumber, and therefore shouldn't be messing around with plumbing stuff in people's houses. She made me feel like I was five years old. The woman would have no heating until her brother in law could fix it the following day. It was the middle of winter. She said she would have to claim her home insurance for the carpet. There was nothing I could offer to help with the situation, absolutely nothing. I apologised time and time again. Once her daughter left, I fixed the border on and cleared my stuff up. When I was getting ready to go, she came through to me with a hand full of a wad of notes. If I remember correctly, the job was worth about £250 to me, and to her gratitude she was still willing to pay me. But I couldn't possibly accept it! I explained that due to my error, I wasn't able to accept the money, and she should use it to pay her insurance excess, and treat herself. I apologised again and left. Since that day, I have never once removed a radiator to paper behind it.

Obviously, my confidence took a bit of a knock after that job. They say that it takes a load of good jobs to build a good reputation, and only one bad job to ruin a good reputation. So far, that was the only real disaster that I had on a homer. I think I was lucky that it didn't harm my reputation that I know of, but I certainly didn't get any more work off that lady. It was a real shame as well because I had done her kitchen before that, and barring the fact I wrecked her living room, if that hadn't happened she would've been well chuffed with the finished result. Looking back, and re-living it all while typing this, I still go red and cringe at the thought of it all. So, there I was, feet firmly back on the ground, back at the drawing board, it was important to get straight back on the horse, but I would never try my hand at plumbing again! It was a week or two before I was doing a homer again, and I always had that disaster in the back of my head, it has never left me. I've seen and heard of people dropping paint pots on carpets, or kicking over a tin, but thus far I have been lucky enough to never have that happen to me. I have woke up sweating a few times after dreaming that I have kicked over a tin of gloss on someone's carpet, and I'm never happier to realise I'm dreaming.

So, I continued through second year, plodding away, and trying to improve every aspect of my work. My thoughts had started to turn to what would happen to me, and Ryan, in third year. The deal was, after finishing SVQ level 3 in 2nd year, 3rd year at college was optional. Optional as in if it suited the student and the company was willing to pay for it. The lecturers at college had been asking if we were to attend, obviously they canvassed everyone, in order to maximise their class numbers. Davie had always promised if we stuck in and did well, then he would *definitely* be sending us back. I kept occasionally mentioning it, and the grants available, throughout the year, and he always responded positively. So it looked as if I would get the opportunity to do advanced craft, which made me pleased. The work at college was getting more and more into the decorative stuff. The unit we were currently working on was "Decorative Skills" and that comprised of Stencilling, Broken Colour Effects, basic Marbling and Graining, and Free Brush Work which formed basic Sign Writing. I really enjoyed this work, as it was quite artistic, but didn't require having that artistic flare, which I definitely didn't have. My mind was telling me that if anything, I would need to excel in this unit to show that I was worth sending to the competitions. Time was getting near when these would be held, so I was trying to make sure I was noticed to be making an effort. Geoff Jones sat us down one day in the workshop and explained a little of what the competition was about. He explained that two from our class would be selected to work as a two man team in the "craft" competition. There would also be one person from the year above us going to the advanced craft competition. He explained that this competition was arranged by the Scottish Association of Painting Craft Teachers. This was like a professional body whose members were all lecturers in the Painting trade at Scottish colleges. The competition was to be held in Cambuslang College in Glasgow, and it would be in a couple of weeks' time. I was buzzing about hearing about this. I *really* wanted to be involved, this was everything to me. I decided that when I started P&D I wanted to be the best I could be, and this was a big part of it. I just hoped I had shown enough to be picked as part of the two man team? That afternoon we were to be practising free brush work. This involved using signwriting "pencils" (which are actually brushes), and practising painting in shapes to get an understanding and skill of controlling the brush. We were given A2 paper and drawing boards, and instructed to draw a series of rectangles on a line, all a given size. Geoff Jones did a demonstration of how to manipulate the brush into creating a sharp right angled corner, and how to produce a straight line. While we were watching the demo, I couldn't help think that this would be a good skill to indicate how I was placed against the others in terms of being picked for this competition. A brand new skill, which none of us had done before, showing our hand skills, and how we adapt to new skills. This was perfect to show me how I was fairing. Wait a minute... I suddenly realised that's exactly what Geoff was doing as well! He was setting up a task, which he would monitor, and watch and the two best would be picked for the competition! GAME ON! I wasn't sure if anyone else had picked up on it. As I worked away, practising my brush skills, I was aware of Geoff walking around the cubicles looking over shoulders to see the work being produced. "Oh yeah Geoff, come and have a look at these lovely sharp corners" I thought to myself. And so he did. I had produced some pretty neat work, even if I did say so myself! As Geoff came round and looked at mine, I felt pretty confident that he would at least have to consider me. We practised most of the afternoon, and I went away fairly happy that I had done my chances no harm with the neat work I had produced.

It wasn't until a couple of days later when we were leaving class to go for lunch; Geoff asked me and Andrew to wait back. Initially, I thought we were in for a row, and then I remembered the comp. Please let it be that I thought. Sure enough, Geoff explained that he wanted us to be a team that they would put into the competition! I was beaming. Geoff explained that the competition was taking place while we were back at work and we would have to ask permission for a day off from our bosses. And he laboured on the point that we weren't chosen because we were any better than anyone else, but because they thought we could work well together. Obviously Geoff didn't want this causing hassle with the other lads, because potentially there could be some noses put out of joint. We both nodded in agreement, but inside I was thinking "aye right Geoff, you *well* know we're the best!" but, I didn't want to be a big head and decided that the humble approach was probably the best approach. I was absolutely delighted at having been chosen. I considered, and still consider, that that day was a turning point for my whole life.

The next couple of weeks were pretty interesting. I think Ryan would've liked to have been involved in the competition, and likewise, I would've liked him to as well. I told Davie about it, as I needed him to agree to me having a day off for it. He did agree. He never said anything, but I think he was a bit proud at that moment, to think that I'd been chosen from the full class. The days we were at college, Andrew ad I took a bit of stick from the rest of the lads. Any time either of us was asked to do anything, a high pitched rendition of "competition boy!" would be heard from some of the lads. It was given, and taken, in the fun way intended. We never really had any noses put out of joint due to us being chosen, but we were both super wary about making sure we never rubbed it in their faces. As Geoff said, we weren't chosen because we were any better than anyone else. And I think it was credit to the full class that he said that. We were a tight knit group, he obviously could see that, and didn't want us becoming "Johnny big times". I totally understood that, and due to the nature of it, anything could happen at the competition, we could end up totally embarrassing ourselves. When I thought of it like that I started to get nervous. What if we went there and the rest of the teams totally wiped the floor with us?? What if the rest were at a much higher standard? I guess I just had to have faith in Geoff and the lecturers, and more importantly, faith in ourselves.

Andrew was a good painter. We were reasonably close, and got on well. I knew I could work well with him, and being honest, I reckon we were both about the same level of skill and talent. Part of me was really looking forward to it, but part of me was really dreading it. But what has become a lifelong trait of mine; I was being driven partly by fear. The fear of letting Andrew down. The fear of letting Geoff down. The fear of letting our class down. The fear of letting Davie and Ally down. To this day, I'm not sure if the "fear driven" ethos is a healthy one, it may seem a bit nervous, but it seems to have worked so far. I decided just to pick out the parts that I thought I could "brush up" on (sorry), try and improve them before the big day, and do my best. No one could fault me if I did my best.

The Competition

The few days before, I asked Geoff if I could take a signwriting pencil home with me to have a little practice at night, which he duly allowed. I made the effort to practice even for fifteen minutes at night, just to keep my hands remembering how to do it. The night before I was like a superstar footballer before a cup final. I had a long hot bath and early night. I had to be up fairly early as we were leaving Falkirk College at 8am the next day. Geoff had organised our tool kit, and along with the lad doing the advanced comp, we all jumped into the college mini-bus. We started the long journey to Cambuslang College. I had never been there before, not that I knew of, and all I knew was it was in Glasgow somewhere. The journey took about fifty minutes. As we arrived at the college, I remember a single level building, which we had to drive around to get to where we were parking. There were students around, and the road was really tight around the building, at one point Geoff was trying to squeeze the mini-bus past some students and around a corner, when the wing mirror on the bus knocked a student's bag right off his shoulder! Geoff never even noticed he had done it, but the rest of us in the back did, to which we all started laughing. When we eventually Larked up, we grabbed the tool boxes and followed Geoff into the building. There was a small reception, and we stood there until someone showed us where to go. I only realised there was an area of the building higher than one level when we were taken upstairs. As we climbed to the next floor we were greeted by a massive sign written sign which said "Painting and Decorative

Finishes", it had a picture of a wee painter looking up at the lettering with his steps at the side. Quite impressive I thought to myself. At this point the Advanced Craft lad was taken away to his competition area. We were taken through the doors and into a room on the right. It resembled the cubicles we had at our college, but the room had more light coming in. Andrew and I got changed into our overalls, there were already some other students there, looking all tidy in there new overalls. I assumed this was the competition! A short white haired man came into the room and gathered us all around him. He introduced himself as Tom Leffrey. He was a jokey man, who seemed to be a nice guy. Little did I know what part he and this college was going to play in my future... but that will come later. Tom explained what was going to be happening that day, and made a draw to see who was going to work in which cubicle. Andrew made the draw and we were put into our area. At this point I was looking around at the other competitors, trying to work out if they looked like they'd be really good or not, but it was useless. At this point I just wanted to get on with it. Tom Leffey handed each pair an envelope, and told us we could start. Geoff drummed into us that we should read through the instructions thoroughly, make sure we fully understand them, work together to get the setting out done, then split up to do agreed tasks. So, after reading through the instructions twice, we set out on our work. Some pairs were already at work, and this made me feel nervous. But, Geoff assured us there would be some teams which would race away fast at the start, but not to worry, and just focus on our own work. As we beavered away measuring and chalking lines, there were quite a few dignitaries walking around watching us. I felt quite a sense of pride that I was involved in such a cool event. These were essentially the best apprentices in the whole of Scotland for our year, and I was one of them. So, we got our heads down and into work.

Lunchtime seemed to arrive in no time at all, and we basically had a quick bite to eat, drink of juice, and back to work. By this point we had split up the work into different tasks and divided them between us. I offered to work on a massive stencil of some sort of logo, which was mainly setting out and masking off, followed by application with a stencil brush. Andrew took charge of some of the smaller pieces of work. It was really hard work, hard on the brain as well as the hands. By the time 4pm arrived, we were pretty much done. As the time allowed ran until 4.30pm we had made it with time to spare. As I finished off, Andrew had a quick look around the other competitors. When he came back he reckoned that we must be in with a shout as there were some teams not yet finished, and those who were done were pretty similar to ours. We spent the last half hour sharpening up anything we could and re-coating anything that needed it, until we were told by Tom Leffey that time was up.

That was it… It was over…My stressing for the last two weeks was over with. It was quite a relief just to have the test finished. I could feel a little weight lifted off my shoulders already.

When we had cleared up, we were ushered into the college's Board Room, where seats had been laid out and there were cans of juice for us to relax, and unwind. They put a film on a TV for us to watch while the judging was going on. I assumed this may take a while. So, we sat, chatted, and drank juice for a while. I felt physically and mentally shattered. My hands kept going into cramp, and I kept having to straighten my hands out to stop them going into "the claw". It was true to say, it had been a hard shift, and I was feeling it!

In the end I think it took about fifty minutes for the judging, and after that time some men came walking into the room, followed by a photographer. There was a man with chains around his neck who was introduced as the president of the SAPCT. He introduced the others, and then said a bit about the day's events and all the competitors. I know sometimes when I hear people saying that everyone involved should take lots from the event and we are all winners nonsense, but I actually felt like even if we didn't get a place, I was better off for being involved!

So, to the important part. Every pair was called up to receive a t-shirt for taking part, as were all the advanced competitors. We were the back seated. The president man then told us that there was going to be three places in each competition. Our Craft competition was to be announced first.

The President man started to speak "in Third Place – Telford College!

The two lads from the Edinburgh College stood up and walked, to everyone's applause, to the front, where they shook hands and posed with their prize of assorted tools, to have their picture taken by the photographer. It was only now I realised there were a good few people standing up the back, mostly lecturers who accompanied their students from all over Scotland. It was then I saw Geoff, who just winked when he saw me.

"In second place... Lauder College!" we clapped as the two boys from Fife headed up for handshakes and pictures. At this point I felt a little disappointed, probably because deep down I thought we could've been good enough for a place. Andrew looked round at me and said "oh well, it's all or nothing now". Deep inside I knew we wouldn't be good enough to win, but I tried to console myself in the fact I was involved and we didn't embarrass ourselves. The two lads from Fife returned to their seats.

"In first place and winners of the SAPCT Craft Competition…"

There was a deadly silence that seemed to last for ages….

…."FALKIRK COLLEGE!!!"

Andrew looked round at me with a wicked smile on his face! "We did it!!" what happened next was all a bit blurry but I vaguely remember walking up to the front of the crowd with the biggest smile ever, and an embarrassed red face to match. Everyone's eyes were on Andrew and me at that moment, I could hear clapping, the cameras were flashing and we were shaking hands with the dignitaries and the President guy. We were handed a wooden shield, with all the past winners engraved on it, and ushered into position to pose for photographs with the President. At this point I remember panning through the crowd, and my eye stuck on Geoff Jones, his fist clenched, punching the air! That vision makes my skin tingle just recalling it. That vision will be with me forever, hopefully. It was all worth it just to see that! As we walked back to our seats and sat down, I could feel my face reddening again! Neither of us could really believe it. The look on Andrew's face was of pure disbelief, the same as the look of a 7year old child on Christmas morning when their eyes first land on the shiny new bike. I knew how he felt; I couldn't actually believe it myself. The people at the front of the room were starting to announce the winners of the advanced section, but it was all just blurred noise to me. I gave myself a dig in case I was showing bad manners, which brought me back into line. I had all but missed who won third place, and I think second place went to a lad from Telford College, but low and behold; Falkirk took first place again! The lad in advanced had done exactly the same as us! It was a clean sweep! As Andrew and I let out a cheer, the lad got up off his chair and headed to the front to receive his trophy. I glanced round to see Geoff, and there he was again, fist clenched! The hair on my neck stood up. As long as I live, I will never forget that day, it holds many amazing memories, and feelings that I have rarely felt since.

It was fair to say, the tiredness and fatigue that I felt immediately post-competition, were totally gone, replaced by pure adrenalin. Needless to say, the mini-bus ride home was livelier than that of that morning! We didn't arrive back at the college until after 7pm, we said our goodbyes and I drove home. I was totally buzzing to tell my folks the news, and when I eventually did, I could see the sense of pride on their faces. That went a long way to making me happy, and I feel that day went a long way to banishing the sour taste of "university no-go" from their mouths. They listened intently as I told them about the full day, with them grinning widely as I did. At that point, it was definitely one of the best days of my life so far! I couldn't wait to tell my mates, Davie, Ally, the boys at college, everybody! It was well before the days of mobiles and Facebook, so it would have to wait until I met everyone one by one- the old fashioned way!

That evening I met a few of my mates, who were suitably impressed. On top of the wooden shield, which had to be returned, we also received engraved tankards, and a radio (the painters best friend), and a small selection of tools. The radio was basically shit, but I could make good use of the tools with my homers, and it would be nice to keep the tankard. I never had the trophy room from football that I'd hoped for, so maybe painting will do instead I thought.

The next morning at work was a little strange. I was

bursting to tell Ryan, Davie and Ally how I got on. When the van arrived to pick me up, Ryan was already in the van. I was conscious of not ramming it down people's throats, so I thought it best to wait 'til someone asked. Ryan quietly asked in the back of the van, and I quietly told him. I felt a bit like it should've been Ryan there, because we had done this whole adventure together, but that wasn't my choice. He seemed quite happy for us. When we got to the job and jumped out the van, Davie came round the back and said "hiya son, how did you get on yesterday with the college?"

"We won it Davie"

"Ye won? Aw very good son, does that mean the company will get a mention in the paper?"

"eh, I dunno Davie, I'm no sure what happens to be honest?"

And that was it. I thought he would've been a lot happier. One of his "home grown tomato's" had done well at a national competition. Very strange, I thought. Ally had a quiet word with me later to see how I had got on, and I think he was pretty chuffed for me. So, it was back to earth with a bump, any delusion of superstardom that I may have had was dispelled straight away, not that I would've. So, work continued as normal, and I went about my business with my head down as usual. I took a bit of a slagging from some of the men, but I quite enjoyed it. It was good having banter with the men, because it was funny, even if I was on the receiving end. It actually lightened my day, and picked me up. I always thought it was a form of love and acceptance. If they were slagging me, it meant they liked me. That day my focus changed dramatically. It had previously been all building up towards the competition, even from the first day I started, that was my aim. And here I was having won the damn thing, what was next? I decided to get my head down that day, get working away, and have a good think. One of the great things about painting, is you have plenty time to think. Straightening out plans in your head, sorting situations at home, whatever was on your mind? I loved and miss that.

The Aftermath

So, what was next? Well, I decided to get my second year at college finished first of all. There were only a couple of weeks left, and we were on schedule to do that no problem. Then I would make sure Davie was planning to send me back for third year, have a great summer, go back to college, complete my advanced craft and win all the many competitions there were for that! Job done I thought! If only it was that easy! Seriously though, the first step was to make sure Davie was still willing to send us back. My thinking was, seeing as I had just won the competition, which would stand me in an even better position. When I asked he still agreed that both of us would be sent back. Perfect! I could now start planning my assault on 3rd year.

After finishing up at college, I had a little sadness that some of the lads definitely wouldn't be back for 3rd year. It was the end of an era. Most of those lads I never saw again. I have never forgotten them, and think of them often. I have a daily reminder about them, and some of the stories I have told over and over. That might possibly be due to the paint fumes taking effect. That summer on site was fairly good. We were getting more responsibility, and being allowed to do better work. That came with extra hassle, but it was worth it. We were generally being allowed to do most things the tradesmen were, and James, the 1st year lad, was getting most of the shit to do. He, himself, was about to start 2nd year, but there was no sign of Davie starting a new 1st year, so James would still be getting the painful end of the bargain for another year. That summer we worked a lot of smaller jobs, nothing too massive, no really big jobs. The bonus with that was that we moved around quite a lot, and got to see a few different places. We had been in some of the roughest areas, but also some of the nicest. My favourite jobs were usually town ones, but occasionally it was nice to be in the countryside. The whole summer my mind was on going back to college. Winning that competition and tasting success, made me want more. It made me realise that when you hear people talking about a "hunger for success", I finally realised what that meant. I wanted to be involved in the competitions for advanced craft; I wanted to be good at all the stuff Joe Lark showed us at college. Sign work, Marbling, Graining; there were all so cool, and Joe made them look really easy. We had a go at them at times, but never to the same effect. People say that if someone can do something and make it look easy, then they must be really good at it. Although I had learned a lot of skills, and really improved my work, I was still nowhere near that level. I decided to set myself a target; I wanted my name on that trophy, the one which the lad in the year above us had won that day. Obviously, there were no team events this year, but I was confident that I could do it on my own. I knew I had loads to learn, but I had faith in the lecturers, and I knew if I put my mind to it, I was stubborn enough to get to that level. I also knew there were a few advanced competitions, more than for the craft level, so I might have more than one chance. So, the first stage of my target was set, back to work, head down, get learning! I felt like I had it all in place, everything set, and nothing could go wrong.... Hopefully.

3rd Year

August appeared very quickly that year, and it was almost time to go back to college. I had been eyeing my college return for what seemed like ages. I returned from work one evening to find a letter with the college stamp awaiting me. I opened it to find an invitation to return back to college for 3rd year. I put it aside to give to Davie the next morning. When we got to work the next morning I showed Davie the letter. He looked at it and thrust it back to me. "They should've contacted *me* about this, not you!" I didn't make too much about his response as I figured he must've been in a mood about something else. I thought that he would come back to me later to talk about it. But he didn't . As the date approached, nothing was mentioned about college, but I just presumed that was ok. I was due to return on a day-release basis, and the day was a Wednesday. I thought that would break the week up nicely, two days at work, college on a Wednesday, then another two days at work. I happened to be working with Matt's squad that week, and when I was dropped off on Tuesday, I reminded Matt that I wouldn't see him until Thursday. Matt agreed and drove off. That evening, I had been out seeing a couple of mates, I returned home about ten o'clock to get a message from my mum. Matt had phoned and left the message that I "had to appear for work the next morning at the usual time". My initial reaction was that there must be some mistake? Matt knew I was going to college the next day? After a minute of thinking, the feeling of dread filled me up. I phoned Ryan to discover he had had the exact same call. Ryan had taken the call himself, and was told the news that I dreaded; Matt had told him we weren't to go to college this week, or any other week. I was absolutely gutted. I couldn't believe it?! I refused to believe it! As the news sank in I became livid with anger. Ryan's reaction made me even angrier; he was totally calm about it! How could Davie do this to us, to me?! He knew how much this meant to me! He knew that I wanted to be the best! How could he possibly take that away from me? Was it about the money? Did I not explain clearly enough about the grants available? If it was about the money, I was pretty sure Ryan wasn't too bothered about 3rd year, maybe he would just let me go? My head was all over the place. Had the letter that came to me instead of him actually upset him that much? The realisation came over me that he never intended us to go back, nothing had been mentioned all summer. I was *so* angry! I felt like going round to his door and ripping his fucking head off! Two full years I had worked hard for that bastard, and he *promised* me we would be going back. At that moment I fucking *hated* him. The most annoying thing was it was too late to do anything about it. It was nearly eleven o'clock at night. I would have to go to work in the morning and confront him then. Hopefully I could plead my case and make him change his mind. Either that or I would kill the bastard for lying to me and wasting two years of my life.

That night I never slept a wink. My head was working overtime. I was going over how I was going to plead my case. Over and over, thinking about how the conversation might unfold. Then I worried about the consequences of not completing my advanced craft. Being refused further jobs because I never did it. Not being the best I could be. That would be disastrous. It would be like buying an expensive suit to wear and only having old trampy shoes to wear with it. What's the point in wearing it? I was never one that liked to settle for second best, and I couldn't bear the thought of not having completed everything that I could've, and ultimately being a Painter and Decorator that couldn't do every skill associated with it. Again, what's the point? My mind would drift to all the times he promised me, and my folks, that I would get every chance of every training opportunity going, and that I could take these skills anywhere in the world. I thought of those days on that Cumbernauld job, freezing my bollocks off, slaving away with that damn sanding pole, for a measly £9 per day. That was slave fucking labour, but I kept going on the promise of what I would receive in training. That was the only thing that kept me going through that time, the only reason I did it, and now the carpet had been ripped from beneath my feet. I was so angry. At 3am I felt like going round there. I was worried about what I might do the next morning. I was angry that he didn't even have the decency to tell us himself; getting his lapdog to do his dirty work for him. It angered me to the stage I knew I was never going to sleep that night, my blood was boiling. As I tossed and turned in bed, everything from two years of work flashed through my mind. I now realised why so many people thought badly of Davie, he was a snake.

The morning sunlight arrived at my window soon after. I was up straight away. It was only five o'clock. I got up, showered and ready. I figured if I went to Davie's door before he left, maybe ten minutes before, I would have time to say what I needed to. Who knows, maybe he would change his mind and I would make college that day?! Every part of my body hoped so. As I had breakfast I explained to my mum what I was planning. She wasn't happy that he had gone back on his pledge. I was watching the clock until it was time to go. As I walked round I was praying inside that this would work. I was shaking with anger. I walked up the drive and rang the doorbell. I could see the white dressed figure walking to the door through the frosted glass. This was it. The door opened and a stony faced Davie looked at me as if he expected it to be the paper boy. As I started to talk, I was so angry the words got all mixed together. I clearly hadn't practised that enough! "Davie, what was that phone call from Matt about last night? Why aren't we to go to college? This isn't fair Davie, you said we could go? You said I would get the best training?!"

He just looked at me. Eventually he said very slowly "you can take that up with my partner, Mr. Martin" he stepped back and his arm reached to shut the door over.

"This is shit Davie, fuckin' shit. You said Davie" The door shut. Aarrgh!!! How could he do this?!! He obviously wasn't ready to explain his actions. I would have to speak to Matt. As I walked back around to my house I was almost in tears, they weren't far away. My hands were shaking; my head was all over the place. It was everything I could do to stop crying. I've never fully understood people that kick doors and break their own possessions when they're angry, but at this minute I totally did. I wanted to smash that bastard. Evil bastard! Messing with people's dreams how could he?! I gave up a university education to work for that bastard on a promise. A promise that meant fuck all to him. As I waited on Matt that morning, I was ready to give him it with both barrels. Poor Matt, stuck in the middle, taking the heat on Davie's actions. I didn't care, I wanted someone's head on a stick, and it would have to be Matt's.

As his car rolled up, I glared at him through the window. I opened the door and let rip before I even got in. "What the fuck is this all about Matt? How can he do this? He said we were getting all the training Matt?

The fucking night before I'm due back? What kind of fucking Mickey Mouse operation is this? You're his wee lapdog running after him doing his fucking shit!"

"GET IN THE FUCKING CAR!"

I got in still ranting, Matt trying to rant back over the top of me, neither of us listening to each other. I had obviously hit a nerve. I had never seen Matt this angry before. His face was scarlet, but I was giving it the best. I had my finger pointing in his face as I ranted. I can't even remember what I said, but I truly did hit him with both barrels. I heard nothing of what he said back, except "well it's down to us whether you do it or not, and the decision's been made!" as we arrived at Banknock to pick up Sneks, Davie's van was parked at the shop. I felt like running up and punching that big head as I passed by it. But, unfortunately, I could only manage to throw him a massive dirty look as I walked into the shop. Standing in the shop waiting to pay for my paper, I could see Matt standing at the window of Davie's van, talking to him. Obviously I was being grassed on. As I walked out the shop, Davie leaned out the van window and said "get your overalls, you're coming in here!" "Oh fuck" I thought.

Ally was in the passenger seat. Making a statement I didn't go in beside him, I jumped in the side door to the back of the van, slamming the door almost as hard as I could. As we pulled away Davie started to rant. He thought he was being clever by never mentioning my name, or looking at me, while he shouted. I had seen him do it many times before, to others, but I had never been on the sharp end myself. He was shouting random statements about "taking people out of the gutter" and "giving people a life". He obviously thought he had saved me from a terrible life by giving me this amazing opportunity to be a second class painter!! As he shouted I glared at him in the rear view mirror. He never looked at me once. I wasn't going to put up with this shit like everybody else! At one point I shouted back "is that me you're talking to?" but he ignored me. Ally just sat through the whole rant not saying a word, not even motioning one bit. He must've felt so embarrassed. It was a really uncomfortable situation. When we arrived at the job, my heart was still pounding. I decided to get a reaction of my own. I sat in the van until Davie came round to open the door, when he did he was met by me with a cheeky smirk on my face. This obviously hit the spot. He was raging back now. "I think I need to come round and speak to your father tonight about your attitude!"

"That's great Davie, 'cos he really wants to speak to you about how you've treated me!" His face dropped. I didn't think he expected that reply. I think he forgot for a bit that my parents were also involved in the situation, that he had *also* promised them about my training. He never spoke to me for the rest of that day. And he never came to see my dad that night, I know that because we both waited in for him to show, and he never. From then on in, my relationship with Davie was completely different. Looking back, and knowing what I know now, I must've been a right little dick to him! He was probably thinking "Who the fuck does he think he is?" And maybe rightly so? But, and I stand by this, no one should treat people like that, promising the earth, then changing plans at the last minute. It's just not fair on people!

More Bad Times

Every day I dreaded going to work. I would jump into the back of his van every morning, in silence, where before I would give a loud "good morning". When we arrived at whatever job we were on, as we put our overalls on, Davie would dish out the orders, and at the end he would usually say " ... and you; you can clean out the van." My daily routine usually started with cleaning out the van and tidying it, washing the outside of it (sometimes in the pouring rain), or some other menial task which needed done. One of his favourite degrading tasks was to take me to his paint store, instruct me to take a pile of paint tins and move and stack them on the opposite side of the store, only to change his mind the following day and have me move them back. I knew his plan though. He was trying to sicken me off so I would leave. I hadn't done anything wrong, therefore he couldn't sack me. And everything he was asking me to do were "reasonable requests" for an apprentice, so I couldn't complain about it. So, I was stuck in limbo, hating every minute of my work time, detesting being there, and having to do the most degrading tasks, but being stubborn enough to not let him get to me. There were days where I would boot stuff around in the back of his van with anger, but I promised myself never to let him see me angry. Every time he made me do something ridiculous, I just smiled at him and did it. I even started calling him Mr. Tinnie. In a strange kind of way, I felt I was making him look like Cinderella's evil step mum. While the men were working, I would be standing in the pouring rain, washing my masters van! Getting soaked to the bone. It got to the most ridiculous stage, one day he took me to his house and instructed me to cut his grass! At this point, I nearly gave up and lost control, nearly cracking him over the head with a garden hoe. "Mr. Tinnie, why am I doing gardening when I'm an Apprentice Painter and Decorator?"

"Well son, we don't have a lot of work on, so if you don't do this I'll have to pay you off"

"Fair enough" I smiled and picked up the extension for the lawn mower. That day I cut grass, strimmed the edges, trimmed his bushes, and hoed the soil. It had all become that bad. My lowest point came when his wife was away to London to visit his daughter, he had me doing his hoovering and dusting in his house! I had sank to an all-time low, but the rest of the guys were laughing their heads off when I returned an told them the story. They called me "Mr. Sheen" for ages after that! At least I could see the funny side, the saying "if I didn't laugh, I would cry" never seemed more poignant. Davie was playing the game. I had to also play the game, but it was Davie's game. The only thing I could do was learn the rules well, and wait for the ball to come to me. When it did, I had to make sure I was ready to give it a thumping hard kick.

When things had turned sour with Davie, I started to look for another job. I began writing to other painting and construction companies. It was the days before emails, so letters and stamps was my only hope. I had a few replies saying they would store my details, and some didn't even reply. My mum mentioned she knew a guy who was a painter with Ogilvie Construction, a large construction company from Stirling. She knew his wife she said, and would have a word the next time she saw her. I didn't hold up much hope, but it was worth a shot. I never mentioned this to anyone at work, just kept writing letters and hoping. I contacted the C.I.T.B apprenticeship officer, and explained my situation. He had a responsibility to make sure I wasn't being mistreated, but because Davie wasn't stupid, there was nothing to report, except for my un-happiness. He promised to keep an eye out for any companies looking for a third year apprentice, but he didn't hold up much hope. It broke my heart to think of my class, all back doing their advanced craft year, and I was hoovering and cutting grass. I began to feel slightly depressed again, it wore me down eventually, to the stage where I was getting to thinking he may win and I might just leave of my own accord. There was more to life than this, and although I hated to admit it, maybe he was going to win; maybe I was cutting off my nose to spite my face? Maybe I should just cut my losses and leave? I could go to college and do something. But I hated even more, the thought of having wasted over two years of my life, to get nothing for it. It was at this point that my mum had spoken to Tom Fallon. A chance meeting with him revealed they used to go to school together, and that he was in fact the Painting Foreman with Ogilvie Construction. My mum had explained the situation with Davie, and that I was desperate to leave. Tom had told her that they hadn't taken on an apprentice for years, and they didn't have a lot of work on at the moment, but if it did improve, then he would give her a shout. She gave him the house number to call. This gave me a little hope, but I feared it was just this man fobbing my mum off to keep her happy. It wouldn't do any harm though. So, I kept my head down, kept plodding on, everyday hoping for a call for someone to save me. Each night when I got home the first thing I asked was if there had been any letters or phone calls for me... quickly followed by what was for my tea? Usually only the latter question gave me any happiness. The only thing that kept me going through this phase was the constant ribbing from the men. Some of the banter was hilarious. When I went to join them working I would hear "shhhh, watch what you're saying boys, here comes Davie's housekeeper!" it was the only thing that kept me going. "Mrs Mop" was my new nickname and cleaning was my new career!

The days dragged in for me again. I very rarely handled a paint brush or hawk and trowel. A sweeping brush was more my tool of choice these days. When I had cleaned out the van or the store, and was told to return to work duties, I more often than not got the worst tasks available. Sanding woodwork or windows, or using the sanding pole to rub down other peoples taping. Once or twice I thought about doing a "Harry Kirkby" and sanding the window pane out of spite. But now, even more than ever, I had to give Davie no chance to pounce on me. I knew he was watching me like a hawk, waiting for me to slip up, so he could sack me. My sister had a similar experience, and was wrongfully dismissed from a job; she eventually took the firm to an industrial tribunal- and won. I knew Davie had to have good reason to sack me, so I had to be squeaky clean. I must never lose concentration for a moment. If he caught me not working, or doing something I shouldn't be- that would be it, game over, and he would've won.

Life wasn't too enjoyable for a while. I would return from work and fill in my parents of what he had made me do that day. I wisely kept a diary of stuff I did, just in case the eventual industrial tribunal kicked off. To make matters worse, I had been playing amateur football, and tore ligaments in my ankle during the warm up before a game! That meant I had to be off sick for a couple weeks. I was down to "statutory sick pay" which was about fifteen pounds a week, but I didn't care; I had two weeks off without Davie watching my every move. It was bliss! I had the house to myself during the day, because everyone was at work, although my ankle was agony and I couldn't drive or go anywhere, I was happy relaxing and watching TV. Towards the end of the two weeks off, I received the phone call I had been waiting for...

Tom Fallon had called regarding the conversation he had with my mum. He spoke to her again, and agreed to come to the house for a chat. I was so excited! Could this be the end of this nightmare? Would he be willing to take me on? I was excited and nervous at the same time. Tom came on the Wednesday night. He came and sat in the living room with my parents and me. He chatted with my mum about my uncle, and then went on to explain that Ogilvie Construction had quite a lot of work on, and he had considered taking on another tradesman, until he remembered meeting my mum. He thought it may be suitable to see what I was like. I did my best to paint a good picture of all the work I was capable of; painting, taping, artexing, coving, and paperhanging. I also made sure I mentioned the competition from college, but I was nervous about telling him about Davie. I played it down as much as possible, as I didn't want to make myself sound like a trouble maker. I kept it brief, and I think he must've been suitably impressed, as he offered me a start that following Monday! I was absolutely overjoyed to say the least! That night I think I could've kissed Tom Fallon! After he left I was buzzing. I think my parents were relieved for me as well. What was a chance meeting had turned out to be a trump card, all thanks to my mum! There was only one thing on my mind at that point, telling Davie. I decided not to tell him for a day or two, as I was worried that it was going to fall through. There could be something that would stop it, some sort of red tape, or mis-understanding which would stop the appointment happening. It all seemed too good to be true, and I was waiting for something to wreck it all. This was a dream come true for me, but normally stuff like this didn't happen to me.

But sure enough, it was real and true. The phone call never came. I decided on the Friday evening to go to Davie's to tell him. I still couldn't believe it was happening. The nightmare was over. I had won! I played the game, Davie's game, and by his rules. I had learned the rules well, waited on my opportunity, and could now see the ball soaring towards me; I was going to make sure I gave it a right hard thump! I asked my dad to come with me, more so he could see Davie's reaction as well, but partly so he didn't become abusive. I now knew he was a pretty nasty piece of work, and I was quite keen to be very abrupt with him, and really give him a piece of my mind with a few home truths, so I expected a backlash. As we left to walk the short distance I could feel the anger in me. My hands were shaking. I was nervous. I always lived by the words "never burn your bridges" but on this occasion I was certain I would never need the services of David Tinnie again. Walking up the drive with my dad at my side I felt like a captain leading his team out at Hampden, chest puffed out to maximum, and if I had feathers I'm sure my full plumage would've been on show. I knocked the door and took a step back. Through the frosted glass I could see his figure approaching. As he opened the door there was an instant look of surprise on his face. When his eyes saw my dad his look turned to fear. "oh, err, hello there son, how are ye?" These were the nicest words he had said to me in six long months. Purely because my dad was there. "Davie, I've just come to say I'm leaving. And you can shove your job up your arse!" with that I looked to my dad, and turned and walked away. That was it. It was over. As I walked back to my folk's house I thought there was so much more I wanted to say, I wanted to hurt him, not physically, but with words, but when I saw him I almost pitied him. There was no point in making any situation worse. It was over and I had won. That was enough for me.

A New Beginning

It took a few days to sink in that it was actually happening. I didn't realise at the time, but everything that had been happening had really worn me down, and I wasn't until the pressure lifted that I realised how much it had taken out of me. It literally frazzled me. But as it lifted I felt so much pressure go. But that was soon replaced with nerves about starting with Ogilvie. Tom had told me I would be picked up by a van on Monday morning at half seven. The night before I was excited and nervous. It was a new start for me, a fresh start. The only concern I had was that my ankle still wasn't 100%, and I was concerned it may hold me back. I looked out bandages to strap it up tightly in the morning. Here we go again!

That Monday morning I woke early, I had the feeling like when you wake up the morning you're going on holiday. Up really early to go to the airport, at a time that you should be very tired, but instead you jump spritely out of bed. Well, as spritely as you can be with a dodgy ankle. I got dressed and had breakfast. I had cleaned out my tool bag that weekend, and had it all organised and ready to go. When the time came, I went outside to wait. I went early, just in case. Didn't want to have any mis-haps on my first day by missing my lift or anything. As I stood at the front of my house nervously waiting for the van, I thought to myself; I never thought this day would come. Just then I heard a very familiar noise... a very familiar sound of a van starting up. Davie had obviously just jumped into and started his van. Oh my word! He was about to pull out from the back of his house. Oh Jesus! Perfect! I would be sitting on the wall, tools at my feet, when he pulls out onto the road and past me. Oh this was going to be amazing! At that the nose of his van poked out the end of the drive. I prayed he would turn in my direction, he didn't disappoint me! He hadn't seen me as he drove onto the road accelerating. Just at the moment he changed into second gear, his eyes met mine. There were so many things I could've done; waved, flicked a V sign, shouted something... all I did was look him in the eye, with a wry smile on my face, and turn my head to follow him as he drove down the road. It was perfect! That, as they say, was all the closure I needed! I knew his blood would be boiling! Guaranteed, his men would find a raging Davie in the van that morning! And it meant I was smiling for the rest of that day!

Not long after that, a white transit van pulled up. A large man opened the window and asked "are you Jimmy the Painter?"

"Yes I am!" I jumped in the side door and sat on my own. It was a van kitted out with seats to transport people, not materials and tools. Already this was a step up from Davie's van. Sitting on paint tins wouldn't be required anymore. I wasn't sure if the guys in front were painters, but I assumed we would be driving to the yard at Stirling, where I would hopefully meet Tom. We stopped along the way to pick a couple of other men up. It reminded me of that first day going to Glasgow in the van with Ally. But this time I wasn't quite as intimidated. I was nervous, but not as much as that day. When we arrived at the yard, I took my bag and asked the driver where I should report to. On his instruction, I headed for the paint store. Just at that Tom pulled up in his car; he greeted me and told me to wait where I was until the men all arrived. A load of vans all with the Ogilvie logo were coming and going into and out of the yard. All the drivers were giving "the nod" to each other. I was surprised at how many vans there were. I tried to figure out who were painters, but it wasn't easy. I figured people with paint on their boots were dead certs, but I hadn't seen any yet. Tom was speaking to different people who were arriving, and he walked into a workshop full of joinery machines and wood shavings on the floor. In the corner was a door, which he removed a padlock from and went into. Several men followed him and came out with various paint tools and materials, before jumping into various vans and disappearing. This was clearly the big time I thought to myself. A big outfit, that already made Davie Tinnie seem like a tiny company. By 8 a.m most of the vans and workers had disappeared. Tom had vanished as well. He came back to the joiner's workshop where I was standing, and asked if while he sorted out some paperwork, could I clean out his pot of brushes? Not a problem I thought! He came back from his car with a paint pot filled to the brim with various shapes and sizes of brushes, stored in water, some in colours, and some in white. He handed me a flask of white spirit and vanished again. His brushes looked as though they hadn't been cleaned in a long time, so I thought it'd be good to clean them and then remove the excess paint from the ferrules. I would give them the full MOT for paint brushes. I took a Stanley knife from my bag and a scraper and started one brush at a time. I found a bit of wood to scrape them on. When I had finished cleaning and rejuvenating them, I topped the pot up with clean water. When Tom came back I handed him the pot. He looked at the brushes, and then looked at me. "Are they the same brushes I gave you?" we both laughed. I wanted him to see I meant business; I wanted to show him he was right to take me on. He told me to jump into his car, as he was taking me to a job. Here we go, let's have it!

We drove for over an hour. Tom explained that the job was in Rowerdennen, on the banks of Loch Lomond. The rest of the men had gone ahead in the painters' van, but Tom needed to go anyway, to check the job, so it'd be a perfect opportunity for a chat. We talked about painting, football, our families, and quite a lot about Davie. I explained that I didn't want to make myself look like a trouble maker, and I certainly didn't want to paint him as the "evil ex-boss", but, I explained, I just had to get away from him for my own sanity. I explained about the college, and the competitions, and how I just wanted to do well and be the best. I think he sympathised with me. Tom, as I would find out, was a cracking guy. A really nice, down to earth man, with no hidden agenda or plan. What you see is what you get. I liked him instantly. He was funny, loved a corny joke, also had the "Painters' Disease" of forgetting that he had already told you a joke, but I laughed the second time anyway. My initial impression of Tom was that it must be great having him as your gaffer, he seemed so fair. Quite the opposite of Davie. We talked about his squad of men quite a lot. I think he was trying to give me a heads up on what to expect and who to watch out for. On this job there were going to be three men and me. Jack Milne, Jim Wilks and Billy Simpson. Tom said that for the most part the three of them were good guys, and good painters. He told me about his other men on other jobs, they seemed a bit more complex, and I remember thinking at the time. So, hopefully, I was safe enough for the time being on this job, hopefully I could find my feet with these guys and take it from there.

We had driven for almost an hour and a half. We eventually arrived at a newly built "Ranger Station". This was presumably where the rangers would stay while patrolling the area. Tom took me inside and introduced me to Jim Wilks. Jim was around fifty, slightly stout, and about the same height as me. He had a happy, friendly nature, and I liked him instantly. Next was Jack Milne. Jack was a rounded guy who looked like he also carried a fair bit of muscle, with a shaved head, all year tan, and ear ring on his upper right ear. He was the youngest, probably around twenty seven, and again, a nice guy. Billy Simpson was the last. He was closer to mid 50's, slim and around my height. Billy had a bit of a drinkers' redness going on with his face. He was sporting a bit of a sweep over haircut, presumably to hide a spot of baldness. But again, I couldn't fault him, he was very welcoming to me! My initial impressions of all three guys, was positive. But, I still had to watch out; I kept reminding myself of what happened with Davie. That day I spent mostly with Jack, emulsioning rooms of new plaster work. Jack was a cracking guy; we talked away as we worked. He was from Larbert, and still stayed with his elderly mum, and he did a bit of door security at the weekends in pubs around Falkirk. I didn't think I recognised him, but mostly it was in pubs I didn't go to. We met up with the other two at lunchtime, where they quizzed me on a few things, Davie Tinnie included. Jim and Billy were both from Denny, so they knew of him, but I tried to keep it low-key. Again, I was away from it so I didn't see the sense in making a fuss. Joe thought he might know my dad, and he went to school with my mum. Billy knew my mum as she worked in the bank in Denny. I felt quite relaxed and comfortable working amongst them. They mentioned a few other guys whom I didn't yet know, so I kept an ear open for any useful information. That day passed pretty fast, and we were soon in the van heading home. I sat in the back with Jack, with the other two up front. All in all, I had enjoyed my first day, and my ankle had held up pretty well. I was really happy. Davie who???

When I got home I was excited to tell my folks about how well it had went. I think that was a massive weight off their shoulders as well. I know it's not easy to watch your child struggle with anything, especially something out of your control. It could tell they were relieved and happy for me. The next morning Tom picked me up in his car, we stopped for another guy called Tony, and Tom mentioned I was wise to sit in the back as the front seat was "Tony's seat", but he smirked as he said it. This was the first clue that Tony might be one to watch. Our first meeting was unbelievable. It was a carbon copy of my first meeting with Sneks. As we pulled up at Dunipace post office for a paper, there was a tall man leaning against the building reading a paper. As I approached, he closed his paper lifted his bag, started walking towards me and *glared* at me menacingly. I thought to myself "oh aye, that wasn't as welcoming". When I returned to the car, Tony was already in "his seat", and we headed towards the yard. Tony was a huge man, mainly slim built but with a little bit of gut, probably heading towards forty. As I sat behind him I couldn't help notice how large his head was! He was a big guy; he and Tom spoke like they had known each other for years. When we got to the yard Tony immediately got out, and headed for a van. Tom told me to wait on Joe, and get in his van to head back to the same job. That morning on the way I asked Jack about Tony. He assured me he was ok, but didn't get along with many people. Throughout my life I have always taken people as they were with me, if they are ok with me, I will be ok with them. Tony had apparently had a fall out with one of the other men, Gibby, and they hadn't talked for a long time. Apparently Tony had been through a bitter divorce and a few folk had the impression he was pretty bitter afterwards. Anyway, I thought if first meeting was anything to go by, if I ended up half as friendly with him as I was with Sneks, we'd be fine! The next few days and weeks were spent working away on various jobs, getting to know more and more of the tradesmen as I went. Again, there was a various mix of types of people, from older guys like Murray, who went to work every day with a shirt and tie on under his overalls, to Gibby, who I didn't think had ever washed his overalls! I was getting to know quite a lot of people from the other trades as well. Because Ogilvie wasn't just a painting company, they also had joiners, bricklayers, plumbers, roofers, and a lot of the people I recognised from Denny. They also had a few apprentices, but I was the only one in painting. I later learned Big Tony was the last successful apprentice they had; the only one after him was a total nightmare. Apparently, he caused so much trouble; they swore never to have any again. There had been a ten year lapse since then, and I was the first exception to break the rule. No pressure then!

After a couple of months I had settled in well. I couldn't believe the difference in general vibe on the jobs. As long as the work was getting done, which it always was, everything was pretty relaxed. I had mostly been involved in what was known as the "small contracts" side of the company. I soon learned the pecking order, and right at the top was Big Tony. He *only* worked for Ogilvie Homes. This was the new build section of the company which built estates full of varying sizes of house. This was apparently the cream of the work, where it was possible to earn bonus money. But, the quality had to match the speed, in order to achieve good money. I was still a third year apprentice, and this was still some way off, but I wanted to be involved. I wanted to be considered, if not *the* best, then certainly among the best. I made that my next target, but before that, I still had my eye on advanced craft.

Jack had it, Tony had it, any joiners that were of college age were doing it. I thought about it, if I'm working well for the company; maybe they'll let me do it? I decided to speak to Tom about it. I asked about the situation, and reminded him how I felt so annoyed about not getting to do it. Tom said that there was a fair chance they would agree; adding, if I was keen to get on, then they would be keen to help me. I offered to pay the cost of the course myself, if they would be willing to let me have the time off? I knew there were grants available though. He only had to consult one of the Company Director's, Joe Haddit. I didn't know him too well other than saying hi to him when he arrived on jobs. I just hoped he had seen I was a good worker, and was worth a punt. Amazingly, a couple of days later Tom came back with the good news, Joe Haddit had agreed! They were willing to let me do my advanced craft in my fourth year, and they appreciated the offer of paying for it, but if other employees got it paid for then I would be no different! Amazing!!! I thanked Tom very much, and made sure I did the same the next time I saw Joe Haddit. I was well happy, slowly, bit by bit, I was righting all the wrongs that occurred under the previous regime. I couldn't believe how open, transparent, relaxed, and fair this company were. It felt like a real privilege to be working for them, compared to how I felt previously. The only point that I picked up on which could be considered negative was that there was a slight level of bitching between the men. This could've been down to the different wages obtainable due to which part of the company a tradesman worked in. plus, working under Tom, he was such a good, fair gaffer, that there was no common "enemy" for the men, so they tended to squabble a little amongst each other.

Again, totally due to having a *good* boss, and also because there was a lot more workers than with Davie's firm. They seemed to be more tight with each other, because they all hated Davie. There were times when I would hear people slagging off Tom as a foreman, and I would think to myself "you don't know how lucky you are mate!" people always tend to forget how good they have at work, especially if they have been in a place for a long time. I still see it now, people who think they are hard done to; when in reality they have one of the best jobs ever! I always tried to keep a check on myself, and I only had to think back to *that* job in Cumbernauld, or the last six months with Davie to remind me of how well off I was.

In reality, I was heading towards fourth year, was enrolled for advanced craft (better late than never), and I was back on top of my game, enjoying my work, and life, and totally buzzing about it all! That full summer, all I could think about was going back to college. I loved summer on building sites, and usually wanted it to last forever, but I knew as soon as it was over, I'd be back at college. We were working on a site in Tullibody, doing a bit of everything, working with tradesmen, doing the outside works on my own, even getting to do some interiors on my own. I liked to think that I was showing the company and my tradesmen that I was a good worker. I always thought that if tradesmen appreciated me, they would request me back with them. And this was happening more and more, people were asking for a shot of me on particular jobs. It was around this time Tom came to me, telling me I was getting moved to another job, and asking how my taping skills were. I re-assured him that I was proficient in all taping and filling, and in fact had been taping before I could paint. I didn't want to sound big headed, but knew I was good at it. After being re-assured by this, Tom explained that I was being sent to a job in Crianlarich. This was a tiny wee place, way up past Callendar; it was a new build fire station. It was to be taped and painted, and they wanted me to be in charge of the painting side of the whole job! I was amazed by this. I was amazed that they trusted me enough. Tom had been to measure and estimate the job, and had intimated it would be ideal for one painter, and Joe Haddit made the decision that he wanted me to do it. I felt honoured! The van would pick me up at my house every morning, as it was an earlier start due to the distance, and I would travel with the site agent and his labourer/foreman. Roll on Monday I thought! Tom assured me all the tools and equipment I required would be there for me, as he was delivering them with the materials the next day. I honestly felt honoured. I was still officially in my third year, and I was being trusted to work a full job, my way, and the way I saw fit, and deliver the level of quality expected. Talk about something to get my teeth into!!

That Monday morning, I was out ready at 6 a.m, and sure enough the van arrived. Driving was *another* Wullie, trusted wing-man/skilled labourer/foreman of the Site Manager, *another* Davie. I had briefly met both of them before, had worked on one of their jobs. Davie was renowned as a crabbit man. He was tiny in stature, and he must've been about seventy, but still fit as hell, and knew his stuff. He didn't suffer fools gladly, was ruthless, and didn't care if he upset people while getting results. He was highly thought of in the company and his reputation as a hard task master preceded him. Tom put it well I thought, describing him as "a little big man". Little in physical appearance, but massive in stature. Wullie was his trusted sidekick, taken with Davie from job to job, known as a real grafter, not scared of work, with hands like bunches' of bananas'. Physically he was tall and slim, pushing sixty himself, but never have I seen anybody graft like this. Facially, I was always reminded of Roald Dahl's "B.F.G", where he reminded me of the illustrations of the big friendly giant. This was going to be some job, I would have a lot of people to convince and win over, but I had been doing that my whole apprenticeship, and it was nothing new to me. Bring it on! Before I had the chance to jump in the side door, Davie was out the van, offering me the middle seat in the front with them. Nice of him to offer, you may think, and it was, but it was the first strike for Davie in showing me who was Boss. He gave me the "bitch" seat, but I was willing to bow down to him, after all he had years of experience I could learn from. This was going to be a very interesting job in more ways than one. As we drove towards Crianlarich, the 6a.m pick up was starting to hit me, and it was hard to stop my head from doing the "nodding dog", something I had always laughed at other people doing. I tried hard not to, but a couple of times I was away. When we arrived at the job it was almost 8a.m, and we jumped out for a stretch off, before being ushered to begin work. Davie was always keen for a sharp start, and he was keen to show me round the job, and familiarise me with the work that lay ahead.

The new fire station basically consisted of a large "garage" area, with really high walls, and a training and living area, which just looked like a few small rooms at this point. The large garage area was all sheeted and ready to be taped. There was a mobile tower scaffold which had been used for the height, and I would use to tape it. The construction was mainly steel frame, which was complete. I was arriving near the end of the job, as the painters always did. Wee Davie had obviously been on the ball with the job, as it was looking great. Tom, true to his word, had delivered tools, materials, and any equipment I needed. Davie showed me the portacabin piece hut. There was an "Owen Pugh" chemical toilet at the side (those things always, and still do, give me the heave). That was basically it. The taping had to be done in all areas, then walls painted, and woodwork, which wasn't yet on, to be brought up in a gloss finish. The one thing that I noticed was, while being shown around, I had been bitten alive by midges! Normally midges come out in very early morning for about 2 hours, then at evening time for the same. It was now half eight in the morning and they were still biting! It was Crianlarich, to be fair though!

So, I was eager to get into some work. I looked out the hawk and trowel, some fibre tape, slightly thinned a bucket of ready mixed filler, and pushed the tower right into the corner. I climbed right to the top and proceeded to apply the tape. I had a radio, decent weather, fresh air, a well-run job, and a large wall to tape. It didn't get much better than this! Davie always ran a tight ship. His jobs were neat, tidy, and well organised. It was clear why Ogilvie kept him working after retirement age. He always made sure that the area someone was to be working in was clear for them, or at least he made Wullie clear it. The only downside for me was that he was really strict on lunch times. I never wanted loads of extra time or anything, but the odd five minutes now and again never hurt anyone. Davie insisted everyone sat in the hut, as did Wullie, and Wullie always got up right on the bell for fear of backlash. As I said, Davie was tiny in stature, and a really old man, but everyone I ever knew was scared of a row from him. He was still pretty intimidating. To me, he just looked like a crabbit wee man; it was the way he glanced over his glasses at things. I never saw him laugh at anything. But I liked him, he had an heir about him, a presence, he too could command respect without even trying. I could well imagine him standing up to the big bosses in Ogilvie, and not caring who he upset. I could well imagine him telling his bosses what to do. So, I certainly wasn't going to argue with him over five minutes at lunch time! I wanted to impress him, I reckon if I got to know him well enough, he would open up to me, and I'd find out what was in beneath there. I figured that Davie didn't open up to many people. Probably the person that knew him best was Wullie. While on that job the odd time we were alone in the van, I'd ask Wullie about Davie, but I don't think even he knew that much about him. He knew the basics though. His wife died a few years ago, along with a lot of his friends, and I got the impression that work was one of the things in life that kept him going. I would imagine, by now, Davie will be a long time dead, I must find out about that. But, I figured the best way to get to know him so he would "let me in", was to impress him through work. I'm always intrigued when I meet someone who "barks", I've quite often found it's a defence mechanism to keep people away. Nobody ever approaches a snarling, barking dog, right? But somewhere in there, there's a dog that loves to be clapped and patted. I saw Davie kind of like that. A snarling, barking dog. A small one though. Maybe a Jack Russell!

So, I set to work, made sure he never saw me slacking, just got my head down and got stuck in. The first couple of days were taken up with first coating the tapes in the large garage area. During the journeys up and down, I was always on the "bitch" seat, so I was perfectly placed to gain any insight into Davie that I possibly could. I tried to only speak when spoken to, mind my language, and be courteous. A few times he asked my opinion on things, and I tried to give sensible, mature answers. I figured if he saw me grafting hard all day, working on my own thinking, and not talking rubbish like a teenager, then he couldn't fail to start to like me. These are generally the things that would impress me with young people these days, and I knew plenty back then that could do none of these! Because I was grafting hard all day, up and down that tower scaffold, quite a few times on the journey home, I was unaware I was doing the nodding dog, until Davie woke me from nearly resting my head on him, with a nudge of his knee. A rather embarrassing situation! Slowly though, I was making progress, mainly just by asking interesting questions. I found out he was a bricklayer originally, and had worked with Ogilvie for over thirty years. He was a tough nut to crack, but I was making a little progress...

Tom would come and visit me every two or three days, or when I requested him to. I think he enjoyed the drive! He mostly wanted to keep an eye on my work, levels of materials, and how the job was coming along. He always seemed to leave happily, especially when he saw how much I'd done. He always had a surprised look on his face. I used to keep a note in a diary, which materials were low, and I'd hand him the note when he came on the job to take away with him. I always kept the materials stacked neatly, in good order, in the container. After completing the taping in the big garage area, it was time to rub it down. The final rub with the "stupid stick" as I had since named it, took just over a full day. I knew I would be doing it, so I made sure the edges were near perfect! Once that was done, I checked what was ready for me in the other half of the building, but the joiners were still busy fitting finishing's. So, between priming any new wood there was for me, I would begin emulshioning the walls in the garage. The mobile tower was a god send during this. I was enjoying working away on my own, but I kept wondering what the other men were doing. I hadn't seen them for a wee while. I also spent a lot of time thinking about college, and the class I should've been in. they would be getting their certificates through the door any day. I was wondering who else would've been back for advanced craft. I also thought a lot about the Davie Tinnie guys. I missed them. Ally, Sneks, Callum, and especially Ryan. Ryan and I had been together since we were four. We went to nursery together, school, high school, and were pals out of school. This was the first time in my life I had been without himby my side. I still spoke to him and saw him outside work, and he always kept me up to speed with what was happening. As the job progressed, Davie started to open up slightly, but I was never going to get inside. I had all but completed my first job as a pretend foreman, and everything had gone smoothly, the only problem was I was going to miss the end of the job because I was going on holiday! I had booked a week in Magaluf with my then girlfriend, and a couple of pals, and I was going to hand over the reins to someone else to finish it. I was gutted to say the least. It almost made me want to cancel my holiday. It had been *my* baby. I had slogged, sweated, and laboured over every part of that building, and someone else was going to come in and gloss a few facings and emulsion a few walls. I knew I had done well with it, had definitely been good value to Ogilvie, seeing as they were still only paying a third year apprentice wage to me. Little did I know, the jungle drums had been beating, as on my return, Jim Wilks passed a comment in the van saying I had been well thought of managing that all on my own. That was all the feedback I required!

Finally, Advanced Craft!

Returning from holiday, the only thing on my mind was college. I couldn't wait to get back and see the staff, get back to learning, and find out about the class I should've been in. my first day back was a Wednesday. This year was going to be different; it was on day release basis, every Wednesday, which broke the week up nicely. When I arrived at college that first day I was met with a shock! Standing at the door of the workshop was James. He was the apprentice the year below me at Davie Tinnie. I couldn't believe it?! After all the hassle I had, most would think he would never entertain students doing advanced again! But here was James. Obviously Davie was trying to rub salt into the wound, and get one final dig at me. It made me laugh actually; at least I'd have someone else I knew. As we waited for the rest of the class to arrive, Geoff and Joe arrived. We had a quick chat and found out there was only James and me! But how could this work? How could they run a class of just two? Would the class even run? It turned out that they were combining the signwriting class with the advanced class, in order to make enough numbers to make it feasible. So, Davie, without even knowing it, had done me a massive favour! If he hadn't sent James, I would never have got to do advanced craft! Thanks Davie!

So, after getting registered, having a bit of induction and a good catch-up with the staff, we got down to a bit of work. It was only Geoff and Joe left at the college, Larry Hatters and Albert Thomson didn't have their contracts renewed, as there was a drop in numbers. I felt a bit sad; as I thought I would never see or hear from Larry again. Thankfully, I was wrong. It felt weird initially, being back at college.

Some of the units we were to be doing that year I have never heard of before. There were also some I had heard of but didn't know what was involved. Glass Gilding, Specialise Wallhangings, Marbling and Graining were all units I knew nothing about, but was keen to get into. All in all, I was ecstatic to be back, and to have James by my side.

I would give James a lift every week, and most Wednesdays we'd end up going to McDonalds for lunch. The only time this changed was when I broke my leg playing football. I was off work for six weeks, but I was desperate not to miss college, so I asked Ogilvie and the college, if it was ok for me still to attend, and do what I could. James managed to get his dad to drop us off and pick us up. It worked out fine. The work was interesting, and at the usual laid back pace. It really took it out of me again. We sat around quite a lot, and that was more tiring than constant work. It was just the nature of the work at college. I kept thinking that I must be in good stead for being sent to competitions. James was a decent painter, but I reckoned I might've had the edge slightly. We were working away well, learning everything from gold leaf to sign work. It was all very interesting, especially when we had Joe Lark. Some of the skills he showed us were amazing. I was enjoying it very much, and was totally appreciative that Ogilvie had invested the money in me. I kept my head down, worked hard, and focussed my eyes firmly on the prize. It was a completely different atmosphere that year. Geoff an Joe were both able to totally let their guard down with us. After all, they knew both of us inside out, as we did them. It was more of a man to man relationship, where in previous years we had been treated like boys. It was nice. But I still gave them the respect they were due, and always used their surnames with Mister in front. I had asked Geoff about the competitions that year, and as far as he knew, there were two. The newest one was "Crown Young Decorator of the Year" and there was the "S.A.P.C.T" competition. Perfect, I thought. That'll do for me! My eyes were firmly focussed on getting to both, and hopefully, doing well. I had total faith in the lecturers, and hoped all would go well.

Later in the year we got word that they were going to send both of us to the first competition. It was to be held at a college in Glasgow. The comp was sponsored by Crown, and had the very grand title of "Young Decorator of the Year". I was as nervous as a turkey in November. It was the moment I had been waiting nearly four years for. I had to do my best, but try not to put too much pressure on myself. I felt like an Olympian, waiting four years for the games to come round, focussing their training on one day, aiming their fine tuning for one day of action. I had told Tom and the men at work, but I don't really think they understood what it was. I wanted this so badly.

On the day of the competition we were driven through by Geoff in his car. We had our tool boxes in the boot. When we arrived we were give Crown T-shirts to wear on the day. We got changed into our brand new overalls, and gathered around the workshop manager to be briefed on the test piece. Then we were away. I took about ten minutes to read through the instructions, making sure every detail was perfectly clear. Some people had already begun. There was a fair amount of measuring and setting out required. I spent about an hour getting that right before I even picked up a brush! Some of the other eleven students had already started applying paint and paper, but I assured myself that the early bird *did* get the worm, but it was the *second* mouse that got the cheese! There was a lot of very neat looking work that day, and as we approached lunch, most people's panels were taking shape. We had a brief lunch, then back to work. It was an exhausting day, and as we approached four o'clock there were some people nearly finished. I was going to require a little longer, but once I did finish the free brush work, I used the remaining time to prune and pamper my effort, carefully wiping off chalk marks, and re-coating anything I could. I achieved, what I thought, was near perfect. Most of the other students had done very similar, with the most varied finish coming in the sponge stippled area. Some finishes were denser than others, but I felt mine sat in the middle of the transparency scale. After all, the essence of broken colour work was being able to see the ground coat. When we finished, I felt relieved, but totally exhausted. It had been a long day. After packing up our tools and removing our overalls we were taken to a room, where, joined by our lecturer's, we were to take part in a quiz. This took up around an hour, while the judging was taking place. I just wanted to get on with why we were all there! After a while, the Crown Paints delegates, returned with the judges. Everyone who took part received a small pack with a couple of tools and a certificate. But it was the main prizes we were all waiting for. I could feel my hands begin to shake and tremble as the bodies assembled at the front of the room. There was a large trophy beside them, along with two smaller ones. Oh well, in for a penny, in for a pound, I thought. I glanced at Geoff and James, and Geoff returned my glance with his usual wink of the eye…

"In third place… from Telford College…"

Oh my, I thought, as my hands shook. The guy from Telford was situated beside me, and I thought our finished pieces were about the same level. He went up, received his trophy and more tools, to everyone's applause. The cameras were flashing wildly as he posed shaking hands with the Crown man...

In second place... from Telford College..."

A third and a second for Telford, which was an amazing achievement? As the lad headed up to receive his prize and trophy, I glanced at James. One thing was sure at this point; both of us weren't going home with prizes. But both of us could still go home with nothing, except our taking part certificate. James looked pretty nervous. I couldn't remember how the lad that took second place had done; it must've been good though. As the cameras flashed away, the lad looked well happy. This was it... All or nothing? I got the strange feeling I had fucked it all up and was going home with nothing.

"And in first place... and the *new* Crown Young Decorator of the Year is..."

The silence went on for what seemed like an age...

"From Falkirk College..."

James and I both sat upright looking at each other...

"Jimmy McKenzie!"

"Yaaaas!" I shrieked. James jumped up and grabbed me and pulled me in for a goal scoring hug. I, in turn, pulled Geoff in for a group hug. I had done it! I had *fucking* done it!

On release from their grasp, amid a thunderous sound of clapping, everything seeming blurred, I walked up to the front of the room towards the dignitaries. I could feel my face stretched in a massive smile, reddening with a childlike embarrassment. When I got there, I reached for the open hand of the Crown man. He grasped my tired hand and shook it vigorously. In a wave of relief, I almost felt like crying. I was handed the trophy, holding it with one hand, and posing for handshake pictures with the other, I could see the camera flashes off the shiny trophy just below my chin. I looked across the room at Geoff and James; both were clapping hard and laughing. In that moment, I totally felt for James, but I could honestly say, this was a victory for both of us. We had been partners all year, and not having got to know him that well at work, I really got to know him well during our time together at college.

As I returned to my seat with the trophy and prizes, I couldn't help feel an overwhelming sense of relief and satisfaction. I had put enormous pressure on myself to win this from the day I started in painting. I wanted to be the best; and my quest to be that had just taken a huge step, but I still wanted to win the S.A.P.C.T advanced comp, which I had won the craft version with Andrew two years previous. The car journey home that day was a quick one. I was in overdrive, and couldn't stop talking. My hands kept going into cramp and doing "the claw". I eventually came back down to earth, but it did take a while! Going to work the next day, I couldn't wait to tell Tom. He seemed really pleased for me, as did Jack and Jim. It was also good for Ogilvie, as the local paper did a piece on my win with a picture, and a mention for the company. Again, as I did when this happened with the competition two years previously, I felt a little like a local celebrity. It felt good, I must admit. People would mention it to my mum at her work, or I would bump into someone I went to school with and they would mention it. Talk about someone's fifteen minutes of fame! My mates were also pretty impressed; it almost became a joke to them.

There really was an amazing release of pressure that day. I had achieved almost everything I set out to do. I had made something of possibly what was seen as a strange choice by many, picking painting over a university education. To be honest I was so glad I had, because it re-assured my own doubts that I had chosen poorly. It almost helped me be more comfortable in my own skin. Before the win, I was possibly still hedging my bets a little, not throwing 100% at it to save face if it did fail. But now, now it was a success; I could take this painting career even further, to the next level. I started thinking more about Geoff, Joe, Larry, and Albert's roles in what I had been doing. I was thinking through the college times I had. So, when painting, I now had something new to let my mind muddle through and sort; could I go and be a lecturer at college? I certainly couldn't think of many downsides to the argument. The only one I kept coming up with was that it was a single place of work. I had come to enjoy seeing different places, some good, some bad, but I never got bored of working on sites anywhere in Scotland. I would be giving that up, but was that a massive thing? Of course it wasn't. After running it through my head for a few days, I decided to speak to Geoff about it, and ask his advice. I was sure I'd need further qualifications of some sort.

The college year, and my college career was coming to an end, along with my apprenticeship. We had one further competition left to compete in, the S.A.P.C.T comp, which was to be held at another of the Glasgow colleges. Again, Geoff drove James and me through to it. It was around this time that I had met a girl who would eventually become the mother of my daughter, my wife…. And also my ex-wife. It was the very early days of the relationship, and where I would normally have been tucked up in bed early the night before, I had a bit of a late one due to the lure of the female form! I wasn't tired that morning, as I was hyped up for it, but I hadn't prepared properly, and I knew it. Once I got started I was absolutely fine. When we walked into the college, I could feel the other competitors looking over, and nudging each other, as if to say they knew I was the winner of the last competition. It felt good, but also a bit unnerving. Although, I knew everyone wanted to beat me, but I would just have to do my best!

The competition piece went well that day; I was hitting everything like I wanted to. I had worked really hard at it and so far, was pleased with my results. We must've been three quarters of the way through, when I stopped, stood back and had a look at comparing my work to the others'. I remember thinking at the time that I was definitely up there among the best ones, and if I keep it going, I could be in with a chance. In part of the test piece there was an inverted "Y" shape which had to be painted in with free brush work around another part of the design, and having completed one leg of the shape, I only had the other to do. I had chalked the lines perfectly, but they were very feint. At the competitions, there were always a good few people walking around watching the action. Mostly these were lecturers from colleges that were there escorting their students, some were dignitaries from paint companies and the like. While up on the step ladder, painting in a section of the shape a man approached and asked if I had set it out properly, and did I know where to stop the line? I took a few seconds to show him the lines were there, although very feint, but I could see them. He went away seemingly re-assured. There was about ten minutes left before the end, and I only had one leg to paint in. As I started it, I couldn't help think how strange that whole conversation was. I didn't know who the man was, he wasn't the workshop manager, and I hadn't seen him before that day. Something didn't feel right about it? Who was that man? Never mind, I thought, let's just get this done and get finished. It was then I realised... I had just painted past the feint line which I had marked out! I had taken the paint too far! Damn! A mistake! How could I have let my concentration lapse and messed up. I tried frantically to fix it, wiping off was an option, but I didn't want to ruin the paint below, painting over with ground colour wasn't an option because it was oil based and would never be dry in time! Aargh, I was so angry with myself! In the end I had to cut the leg off where it was. I knew I had right royally fucked up! I just hoped that it was still good enough work to have a chance. I began to wonder whether that man had a mind game in place whereby he distracted me hoping I would make the error I just had made. If he did, it worked a beauty! I looked around to see if he was still around, but he was gone. I never saw him again that day. I don't know who he was.

As the competition finished I was gutted. In the closing few minutes, all I could do was try to tidy the test piece up as best I could. Standing back seeing one leg of the inverted "Y" shape longer than the other, I knew I had blown it. One minute of lapsed concentration had ruined eight hours of work. I was so annoyed, and only at myself. Looking over the rest of the panel, I honestly thought the work was flawless, but the one mistake stuck out like a sore thumb. My only hope was that there were marks dropped on my counterpart's work. As I packed up my gear I felt my heart sinking. How could I have been so stupid?! Why did I stay out late the night before chasing "skirt"? I hadn't prepared well enough, and possibly got arrogant about it. I hadn't realised at the time, but I had totally under-estimated the competition, the other competitors, and how much they wanted to beat me. Maybe that guy coming up and asking me that question was gamesmanship, it didn't matter. I was responsible, and deep down I knew I didn't deserve to win, even if I hadn't made that final mistake.

At the awarding ceremony, I felt so low. There were glances towards me from other competitors, students who had seen me win at the last comp, and I think they knew I had fucked it up. And they were right, when the results were read out; I was still genuinely surprised to hear my name winning third place! Now that was a result! I was ready to grab my stuff and leave straight after the final whistle, but winning third really humbled me even further. I did take a lot from third place, and I was more than happy with it, but I didn't sleep for days thinking about, and playing over and over in my head, the moment where I forgot about the line I was to paint to, and I pulled that signwriting pencil past it. I still think about it now. It still haunts me to this day. On looking back, I can't remember who won second or first place that day, unfortunately, James wasn't one of them; that would've made it more bearable. But I was still proud to have won third, and I still got a mention in the local paper, just not with a picture. Going back to work the next day, all the men were happy for me, but on telling the story, I could tell they were disappointed. They knew I had high standards, and I just felt I had let myself down a bit. As the days and weeks passed, it still annoyed me. It still does to this day. I guess that'll never leave me. I tried to put it behind me and move on, I had my skills test coming up, and had to focus on that.

The Final Hurdle

After completing my advanced craft, broken legged for some of it, I was overjoyed. It had seemed to be the pot of gold at the end of the rainbow. I could never quite reach it. I felt I was never going to get the chance to do it, but thanks to Ogilvie, I was there. Their great attitude towards learning, and getting on with business, had allowed me, and paid for me, to get right back on track to having had a premium apprenticeship with all the trimmings! The only hurdle left was my skills test, and then see my time out 'til the official date that I started. I had the letter through about the skills test. It was to be completed at Lauder College, in Fife. It could only be done at a registered C.I.T.B testing centre, and Lauder was the closest one. I called Ryan to see if he had received a date, and he had, the same as mine, also at Lauder! I could see a road trip! I made sure I knew where to go by having a wee drive through one Sunday, before the test, just so I wasn't getting lost on the day. It was a two day test to include painting, paperhanging, and some selected various tasks. I felt pretty confident about it, surely I couldn't do so well in the competitions and struggle on the skills test? I hoped not.

That morning we left around 8a.m for Fife. I picked Ryan up, and we set off, just like the old days. As we drove through, we discussed the test, work, both companies that we worked for, and plenty of other stuff. Ryan was getting a bit of a hard time from Davie, for whatever reason, and he had been under a fair bit of pressure from him. He saw the whole story that I went through with him, first hand, and I tried to re-assure him that he should look elsewhere. Ryan re-assured me that James being sent to do his advanced wasn't Davie having a dig at me; he was having a dig at *him*. After I left, unknown to me, Ryan had also kicked up a bit of a fuss. The realisation must have finally hit him, that he actually wasn't getting to do it, and it was a serious problem. Davie must've taken offence to that, but kept quiet, and then the following August he sent James, still with no intention of sending Ryan! I couldn't help think, that would've been me, if I hadn't got off my arse and found another job, ahem cough cough, If my mum hadn't. But seriously, I would've been still in the same position. Thank God I was lucky enough to find Ogilvie. But it still annoyed me that Davie was getting away with being so nasty to employees. It wasn't fair for people to put up with that sort of behaviour, especially from a company. It was no surprise that most people eventually moved away from working with him.

Anyway, that morning we arrived at Lauder College, we were directed to an outside building which was situated at the back of the college. As we went in there were a few lads standing around. They were obviously there for the same test. A man eventually arrived, and positioned us into individual cubicles. I was working next to Ryan. I had a pleased feeling when I knew I was close to him again, I had missed having him beside me. We were briefed on the test. There was a "fire-place wall" which had to be finished in vinyl paper, a varnish door, a gloss door, an emulsion wall, and some facings and skirtings which were to be glossed. It was a two day test, so I decided to get all the painting done, so it left just the paperhanging to be done the next day. We both worked hard that day, beavering away in our cubicles. Part of the test was on cleanliness, so the floors had been freshly painted with red floor paint, which would show up how successful our use of protective sheeting was. If we never covered the floor properly, and then there would inevitably be paint spots on the floor for all to see. I made sure my dust sheets were well placed in order to protect the gleaming red floor. This was supposed to re-create someone's house with a lovely carpet which had to remain spot-less! The first day passed without any major problems. I worked right up to the allocated time. I had completed everything I wanted to, and more. I had enough time left that day to erect my paste table and cut my lengths for the next day. I was really happy with what I had done. That would give me a good start for the next day. Ryan had also done very well. He was just finishing his skirtings with gloss paint as the buzzer sounded to end our day. By all accounts he had to rush a little to get all his painting finished, and he admitted himself in the car on the way home that he had completed his skirtings quicker than he would've liked. As we drove home that evening, we were both confident that the work we had produced was good enough to pass the test, our last obstacle on the way to becoming fully qualified tradesmen.

The next morning, I picked Ryan up as normal, and we headed back through to the college in Fife. We were allowed into the test area when the manager opened the door to us. I had a quick check through my work from the previous day, just to make sure there were no runs or other defects which had occurred after us leaving. All my work seemed fine. It was around that time that I heard a shriek coming from Ryan's workspace. As he had hastily slapped the gloss on his skirtings the day before, he didn't have time to go back and check for runs. But what had occurred once we left were little puddles of white gloss on the gleaming red floor at the corners of the mitred skirting. Clearly he had put too much paint on, which had run so far it gathered on the floor and had begun to harden. When I went in to investigate the shriek, my eyes were immediately drawn to the little pools. I was gobsmacked. How could he have managed that?! In its current state, the test was a failure. Ryan would have to do something to fix it. He found the workshop manager and asked for his advice on the matter. After a bit of arm folding and un-folding, and some very sharp intakes of breath, and possibly even a snigger or two, the man told Ryan his best bet was to touch up the white gloss on the floor with the red floor paint, of which there was a tin sitting on the bench. Ryan hurried to get the offending areas touched up, but to his horror, the red was a slightly darker shade. It looked even worse than before! He clearly hadn't noticed when it was in the tin, neither had the manager. It was a close shade, but as soon as he put it on the floor, the adjacent colour was obviously lighter. This was a confusing period. He wondered if the red paint may lighten a bit on drying, and it only appeared darker as it was wet? He wondered that until he spoke to and showed the manager. He confirmed what Ryan and I feared; it was a different shade! The wet paint was impossible to clean off, as was the white. He would just have to leave it and hope he would do well enough in the rest of the test to pass. He worked super hard on making his paperhanging perfect. As did I. There were no real complications for me. And I finished well before my allocated time. In fact, it only took me an hour to complete the paperhanging part. I spent a little time checking over all my work, making sure everything was 100%. By eleven o'clock I was ready to head home, but I had to wait on Ryan. He had also done well with his paper. It was a real shame the skirtings took the shine off his work. As he completed, I think we both knew he wasn't going to pass. We headed home that day, I was quietly confident that I would pass. But I was gutted for Ryan. He was pretty quiet on the way home. I think he was going through similar emotions as I did when I fucked up the competition a few weeks previously. I could tell he was running it through his head over and over, torturing himself with it.

A couple of weeks later Tom Fallon came to me on a job to tell me that I had passed my skills test. Although I knew I had done well, I was still a little concerned about not passing. Luckily, I had done enough to pass, and that was all I needed to know! Unfortunately, as predicted, Ryan failed his. He went on to re-sit it, but unfortunately failed again. To this day, Ryan never re-sat the test for his third time, and he soon after quit Davie Tinnie's company in a big bust up over his wages. Ryan soon went to work for another local firm, as an Aimes Taper, at which he is still working today. Still with no formal qualification from his time at college, but with all the skills he picked up along the way. I still see Ryan around our home town sometimes, and whenever we meet, it's like we have never been apart; the mark of a true friendship.

As for me, I was working in a church in Stirling. We were redecorating the ceiling and walls. It was August 18th, my 21st birthday. Already, this was a big day; a person only turns 21 once! Tom Fallon had arrived unexpectedly on the job. He had been talking to Jack and Jim Wilks about the work being done, and then he came over to me. After a minute of chit-chat he announced "Your time is out today son, as of tomorrow you are time-served. I got a letter this morning from SQA." I couldn't believe it! Not only was it my 21st birthday, but the end of my apprenticeship had coincided with it! What were the chances of that?! I was amazed, and thrilled! I asked Tom if it would be ok to take Jack and Jim to a pub at lunchtime for a beer to help me celebrate. I asked if he would like to join us?

Unfortunately, he had to be away soon, but said it'd be ok as long as it was just one drink. That lunch I took the two men, men who had been instrumental in getting me settled in to life at Ogilvie, they had taken me under their wing, shown me the ropes, and helped me when I needed it. I couldn't believe how these important days had coincided. But I kept thinking, it was meant to be. All my hard slog, all the difficult times with Davie, they were all being washed away and forgotten with every mouthful of lager I drank! That day I drank my beer and celebrated with two people who had been my tradesmen, became colleagues, and most importantly, friends. Afterwards we returned to the job at the church. I worked away all afternoon with a warm glow of satisfaction. I had come a long way since that morning I had jumped into Davie's van. I had been through some very difficult times, times which would last a lifetime in memory. That afternoon I considered the lows and highs of the past four years, and how they had affected me. Finally I felt free. I felt at the end of a journey. For a moment I pondered on that thought. But it was really only the beginning of my journey. There was more, much more, to come. Highs, lows, successes and failures. It had been a bumpy ride so far, one which I was glad to come out the other end of the tunnel. It had taken a lot out of me at times, but nevertheless, I had made it. I thought about Davie, Ally, Matt, Davie Mullen and others. All had had a part to play in my story, and I would've liked them to share in my success, but they mostly had become figures I would never see again.

So, what became of me? A successful tradesman? A lecturer at college? A company owner? Well, all these questions will be answered in good time, but for now I was just happy to have survived, and emerged as a graduate, from the "University of Life". There was going to be plenty of time to think about what was going to happen in the future. For now, I just wanted to go and be a tradesman, and a good one at that! I could now go anywhere in the world with this qualification, and make money. I could work abroad, on oil rigs, or even start my own firm. This was going to take a bit of thought…

www.ingramcontent.com/pod-product-compliance
Lightning Source LLC
LaVergne TN
LVHW090116080426
835507LV00040B/902